International
Microcomputer
Dictionary

International Microcomputer Dictionary

Berkeley • Paris • Düsseldorf

Cover by Daniel Le Noury

Library of Congress Card Number: 81-51133
ISBN 0-89588-067-9
First Edition 1981
Printed in the United States of America
10 9 8 7 6 5 4

Acknowledgements

The text of this book has undergone substantial revision and been shown to many people, the final form benefitting from the comments and suggestions of a l. We are particularly indebted to the following contributors to the foreign language section: Luc Dekeyser, Jesus Gulnea, Bjarne Hansen, Harold Lawson, Romuald Marczynski, S. Richard Mateosian, Veljko Milutinovic, Lars Monrad-Krohn, Ryoichi Mori, Antonio Alabau Muñoz, Alex Para, Giovanni Seghezzo, Torstein Skard, F. Vajda, Pat Wells, Vllaznim Xhiha, and Rodnay Zaks.

Table of Contents

Introduction

This dictionary provides a convenient reference for all those involved or interested in the microcomputer field. It is divided into four parts.

The first part is the dictionary proper. It consists of alphabetically arranged definitions of the most common terms and acronyms to be encountered today in microcomputer circles. Also, as an aid for those who must speak microcomputer acronyms as well as understand them, it includes an explicit pronunciation for those acronyms that are not simply read as the letters that make them up. For example, no pronunciation is given with the "BCD" entry because this acronym is always spoken "Bee Cee Dee." On the other hand, the "EBCDIC" entry carries the pronunciation "ep-si-dick," which could scarcely be inferred from the letters of the acronym itself.

Recognizing that many terms in current use throughout the microcomputer community are neither words nor acronyms, but numbers, we have also included "The Numbers Game," a numerical list of such numbers or codes. The list is short, because we have confined ourselves to numbers which are, or will soon be, part of the general microcomputer vocabulary. The Numbers Game is not intended to be a substitute for, or even a key to, those vast handbooks of part numbers and data sheets which are the special province of the microcomputer hardware engineer.

The second part is the International Microcomputer Vocabulary, a list of common microcomputer terms with their equivalents in ten European languages. The Vocabulary is organized into two sections, each consisting of the English followed by the equivalent words in five languages. The languages occur in alphabetical order: Danish through Hungarian in Section One, Italian through Swedish in Section Two.

The third part consists of some Standards and Specifications: signal specifications for the RS-232, GPIB and S-100, and ASCII and hexadecimal digit conversion tables.

The last part is a current collection of names, addresses and telephone numbers of prominent Microcomputer Companies: suppliers of systems and components. A list of informative periodical publications is also included to help keep pace with this fast-growing field.

PART ONE

Dictionary: Definitions and Acronyms

A Accumulator. *Also:* Address line. *Also:* The hexadecimal symbol for the decimal integer 10: $A_{16} = 10_{10} = 12_8 = 1010_2$.

Å Symbol for Angstrom, which equals 10^{-9} meter.

abort The process of terminating a program in an orderly fashion and returning control to an operator or operating system.

absolute loader A program to load a program into memory at fixed numerical addresses.

absolute value The magnitude of a number expressed as a positive number. Denoted by enclosure in vertical bars (|). Thus, if a number x is positive or zero: $|x| = x$. If x is negative: $|x| = -x$.

A-bus The primary internal source-bus to the ALU in any processor.

ac Alternating Current

AC ACcumulator

ACC ACCumulator

access time The time required to fetch a word from memory.

accumulator A special-purpose register in which the results of an ALU operation are placed. There may be more than one accumulator in a central processor. *See:* ALU, CPU.

ACIA Asynchronous Communications Interface Adapter. Motorola's term for a UART.

ACK [*"ack"*] ACKnowledge character in ASCII, a 06_{16}.

acknowledge A control signal used to complete a handshaking sequence. The ACK signal indi-cates that the information has been accepted.

ACM Association for Computing Machinery

acoustic coupler A device for connecting the telephone handset to data communication equipment (DCE) such as a modem linked to a computer.

ACT ACcumulator, Temporary (in the 8080 microprocessor).

A/D [*"A to D"*] Analog to Digital. Conversion from a sensor's analog voltages and currents to the digital representation used by computer systems. This is so computers can process data sensed directly from the external world.

Ada A high-level language sponsored by the DOD originally for real-time systems programming.

ADC Analog to Digital Converter

ADCCP Advanced Data Communication Control Procedures

adder A unit that performs binary arithmetic in a processor.

add-on Circuitry or system that can be attached to a computer to increase memory or performance.

address A number indicating the position of a word in the memory. 16-bit addresses range from 0 to 64K.

address mark A special 8-bit code (in fact, 8 bits for clock, 8 bits for data) used at the beginning of specific fields on a disk track, such as index, ID, data, deleted data.

AIM-65 A single-board 6502 microprocessor-based computer made by Rockwell.

ALGOL [*"al-gall"*] ALGOrithmic Language. An early (1960) high-level programming language with a structure known as context-free.

algorithm Step-by-step specification of the solution to a problem terminating in a finite time. A problem is stated, an algorithm is devised for its solution, and the algorithm is then represented by a flowchart. The flowchart is finally translated into a program.

alphanumeric The set of all alphabetic and numeric characters.

alterable memory A storage medium that can be written into.

alternating current Any signal that varies with time can be considered alternating current. It usually means that the current actually changes polarity with time.

Altos A manufacturer of pre-packaged Z80 microprocessor-based business computers.

ALU Arithmetic Logic Unit

AM Amplitude Modulation. *Also:* Address Mark.

AMD Advanced Micro Devices, a manufacturer.

AMI American Microsystems, Inc., a manufacturer.

ampere Unit of electrical current related to the actual number of electrons moving past a given point per second.

amplifier A device or circuit that increases the power of a signal.

AN/UYK [*"ann-yuck"*] Army Navy/ Universal digital computer.

analog Having a continuous range of voltage or current values. *Contrast with:* digital.

analyser, analyzer Any device that monitors a component, board, or system and presents the monitored data for review. *See:* Digital Analyzers.

AND Term for a logical operation defined by the rule: if A AND B are 1, then C is 1, otherwise C is 0. The AND of 10110111 and 10000100 is 10000100.

ANSI [*"ann-see"*] American National Standards Institute

APL A Programming Language. A high-level programming language invented by Kenneth Iverson, and used for algorithmic interactive programming.

append To add to the end of a structure, as in appending a character to a character string or an item to a list.

arbitration Management of competing claims of multiple systems or processes for a limited resource. Especially bus arbitration, which is the allocation of a system bus among the various subsystem components, such as CPU memory, disk controller and other external devices.

architecture The particular selection, design, and interconnection of the principal components of a system. In an MPU: the number and function of registers, the instruction addressing modes, and the bus structure and timing.

arithmetic logic unit The element which can perform the basic data manipulations in the central processor. Usually the ALU can add, subtract, complement, negate, rotate, AND and OR.

arithmetic statement An instruction specifying an arithmetic operation.

ARQ Automatic ReQuest for repeat

ASCII [*"ask-ee"*] American Standard Code for Information Interchange. This character code is used for representing information by most non-IBM equipment. *See:* Baudot, EBCDIC, ISO.

ASCII keyboard A keyboard which includes keys for *all* of the characters of the ASCII character set. Generally includes three cases for each alpha character: upper case, lower case and control (CNTRL).

ASR Automatic Send Receive. A terminal having, in addition to a keyboard and a printer, an automatic reading and recording device, such as a cassette tape unit or a paper tape reader and punch. *Contrast with:* KSR.

assembler A program which takes the mnemonic form of the computer's language and converts it into binary object code for execution. It acts as a compiler for machine language. *Compare with:* compiler.

assembly language A hard-ware-dependent symbolic language, usually characterized by a one-to-one correspondence of its statements with machine language instructions.

asynchronous An event or device which is not synchronous with the CPU (or other process) timing.

ATE Automatic Test Equipment

AT&T American Telephone and Telegraph

Atari A prominent manufacturer of microprocessor-based games and personal computer systems.

attenuation Loss of amplitude of a signal.

AU Arithmetic Unit. *See:* ALU.

auto-answer A modem capable of automatically establishing a telephone connection between a computer and a remote device when dialed over the telephone network.

AV AVailable

B Bus line. *Also:* The hexadecimal symbol for the decimal number 11:
$$B_{16} = 11_{10} = 13_8 = 1011_2.$$
Also: Second accumulator of the Motorola 6800 microprocessor.

background program In a multi-programming environment, a low-priority program which operates when the processor has nothing else to do.

backplane The physical area where the boards in a system plug in. It usually contains the buses of the system either in printed circuit or wire-wrap form. Also called a motherboard.

backup copy A duplicate copy preserved (usually on a different volume or medium) in case of loss of the original data or program.

bank A logical unit of memory (usually 64K).

bank select A method of extending a computer's RAM memory by selecting one of many memory "banks," all of which respond to the same addresses.

bar code The consumer product information code which uses combinations of bars of varying thicknesses, designed to be read by an optical wand.

base register The register containing base address for indexed-type referencing. The final effective address is obtained by adding a displacement to the contents of the base register. *See:* index register.

BASF Badische Anilin und Soda Fabrik, a manufacturer of magnetic storage media.

BASIC [*"basic"*] Beginner's All-purpose Symbolic Instruction Code. A popular computer language invented at Dartmouth for educational purposes. An easy-to-learn, easy-to-use language, it is most similar to Fortran. It is available now on almost all microcomputer systems in varying degrees of completeness. There are tiny BASICs, which have just the bare essentials, regular BASICs, which are usually some form of Dartmouth BASIC, and super BASICs, which may incorporate features from other languages. There are often serious compatibility problems between various BASICs.

batch processing A mode of processing in which any program submitted to the computer is either run to completion or aborted. No interactive communication between program and user is possible.

battery A device for producing electrical energy by chemical means.

battery backup A method for retaining the contents of volatile storage during a power failure by providing an auxiliary power source from batteries.

baud The number of bits transmitted per second. Actually, the binary units of information transmitted per second. Teletypes transmit at 110 baud. Each character is 11 bits, and thus the TTY transmits 10 characters per second.

Baudot An older communications code, named for the man who invented it, and used for 5-level (hole) teletypewriter and telex machines. Other codes used are ASCII and EBCDIC, which are 8-level codes.

baud rate generator An oscillator, usually adjustable, providing clock signals for connection of a peripheral. Typical rates are 110, 300, up to 9600 baud.

BB Burr Brown, manufacturer of D/A and A/D products.

B-bus The second source-bus to the ALU in a 2- or 3-bus processor.

BCD Binary Coded Decimal. A 4-bit binary representation of the

10 decimal digits 0 through 9. Six out of the sixteen possible codes are unused, requiring the use of a "Decimal Adjust" instruction for correct binary addition. 1 is encoded as 0001, 9 as 1001. Two BCD digits are usually packed in a byte.

BCP Byte Control Protocol

BDLC Burroughs's Data Link Control

Bell Laboratories Research laboratories in New Jersey which originated many prime discoveries in the electronic and computer fields.

benchmark program A specific program written to calibrate the speed of a computer in a well-defined situation, or type of computation, e.g., scientific "number crunching," sorting, or compilation.

bidirectional Data flow may go in either direction on a wire. At each end of the wire there are transceivers to both receive and transmit. Common bidirectional buses are tristate or open collector transistor-transistor logic.

bidirectional printing Alternately printing in either direction. A line printed left-to-right is followed by a line printed right-to-left. This avoids the usual carriage return delays, greatly increasing throughput.

binary counter An electronic device which outputs a sequence of ascending or descending binary numbers.

binary number A representation of an integer as a sum of

powers of 2, using a sequence of 0s and 1s.

binary search A technique where the search interval is divided by two at every iteration.

BIOS Basic Input/Output System. A part of the CP/M operating system which manages serial peripherals.

bipolar A technology of integrated circuit fabrication which uses transistor switching elements based on majority carriers for switching and amplification. *See:* MOS.

bistable Describes a device which is always in one of two possible stable states.

bistable multivibrator Flip-flop

BISYNC [*"by-sink"*] Binary SYNchronous Communications protocol

bit A contraction of binary digit. A bit is a 0 or a 1. Bits are universally used in electronic systems to encode information, instructions, and data. Bits are usually grouped in larger units such as nibbles (4), bytes (8), or words (16, 24, 32, 86 or more).

bit-parallel Describes a method of data transmission in which every digit of a binary number is sent simultaneously over a separate wire.

bit-slice A vertical slice of a computer. This component constitutes an n bit slice of a traditional CPU, minus control. Usually n = 4. A bit-slice implements a complete data path across the CPU, including multiplexers, ALU, shifters, registers, and accumulator(s).

blanking   Not displaying a character on the CRT ("blank beam").

block   A physical unit of information in a logical record. Block size is usually expressed in bytes.

BNPF representation   An older data encoding format for PROM programmers using the characters B = beginning, F = finish, N = negative (1), P = positive (0). For example: the byte 11110000_2 is represented as BNNNNPPPPF.

board, breadboard   The fiberglass or pressed paper sheet used for mounting the integrated circuits. Interconnections may be wire-wrapped, soldered, or printed on the board. The term breadboard refers to a prototype circuit and dates from the time when radios were made on mother's breadboard.

board-tester   A device, usually computer controlled, which performs electronic tests on printed circuit boards.

Boolean Logic   Named after George Boole, who defined an algebra of logical operations such as AND, OR, and NOT, on the two values true and false.

boot   To use a bootstrap. Generally used to describe starting up a computer. *See:* bootstrap.

bootstrap   A program used for starting the computer, which usually clears memory, sets up I/O devices, and loads the operating system from ROM, disk or cassette.

BOP   Bit-Oriented Protocol

bouncing   The vibration of mechanical switch contacts after closure, which results in a short period of intermittent conduction.

bound   See: processor-bound, I/O-bound.

bpi   Bits Per Inch. Used to specify the density of data recorded on tape or disk.

branch   An instruction identical to jump, i.e., one causing a transfer of control to another program sequence.

breakpoint   A point at which the processor will stop a program sequence and dump the current machine status. It may be implemented with hardware, software or a combination of the two.

BTAM   [*"bee-tam"*] Basic Telecommunications Access Method (IBM term).

bubble memory   Memory utilizing microscopic magnetic domains in an aluminum garnet substrate. Present memories have 92K bits per device. Future devices should boast better than 1 million bit storage density per chip.

buffer   In hardware, a device which restores logic drive signal levels in order to drive a bus or a large number of inputs. In software, any memory structure provided ("allocated") for the temporary storage of data. *See:* driver.

buffering   The delaying and temporary storage of data in a data communications path.

bug A mistake. Eliminating the mistakes from a program is known as debugging. *See:* DDT.

bulk storage Large capacity data storage, generally long-term.

burn-in A phase of component testing where basic flaws or early failures are screened out by running the circuit for a specified length of time (such as one week), generally at elevated temperatures in some sort of oven.

bus Path for signals having a common function. Every standard MPU creates three buses: the data bus, the address bus, and the control bus.

bus controller The unit in charge of generating bus commands and control signals.

bus extender A device which allows additional cards to be plugged into a computer's bus.

bus termination An electrical means of preventing reflections at the end of a bus that is only necessary in high-speed systems or poorly designed low-speed systems.

byte A group of 8 bits. A byte is universally used to represent a character. Microcomputer instructions generally require one, two or three bytes. One byte has two nibbles.

BYTE A well-known magazine for computer hobbyists.

C Carry bit. *Also:* Clock. *Also:* The hexadecimal symbol for the decimal number 12:
$$C_{16} = 12_{10} = 14_8 = 1100_2.$$

Also: A high-level programming language developed at Bell Laboratories, associated with the UNIX operating system.

cache A high speed buffer memory used between the central processor and main memory. The cache is filled at medium speed from main memory. Instructions and programs can operate at higher speed if found in the cache. If not found, a new sequence of instructions is loaded from main memory.

CAD Computer-Aided Design

CAI Computer-Assisted Instruction

call Instruction used to transfer the program execution sequence temporarily to a subroutine or subprogram. Upon termination of the subroutine, execution is resumed at the instruction following the call.

call by reference A subroutine or procedure call in which the addresses of the parameter's storage locations are passed to the subroutine.

call by value A subroutine or procedure call in which the actual values of the parameters are passed to the subroutine.

CAM [*sometimes* "*kamm*"] Content Addressable Memory. Associative memory, addressed by contents rather than position.

CAMAC [*"kam-mack" or "kay-mack"*] Computer Automated Measurement And Control. The IEEE 583 instrument interface standard, which is a set of physical and electrical standards used for potentially high-speed instrument interfacing in the nuclear industry. It is preferred over IEEE 488 in many industrial environments.

card A printed-circuit board.

card cage A rack designed to support the printed-circuit boards in a computer.

carriage return A standard type-writer key causing the printing element to move back to the beginning of the line. A separate line feed must be supplied to move the paper up. A carriage return is frequently interpreted by the microprocessor as meaning end of line or end of command.

carrier A frequency used to "carry" information, which is modulated to denote 0 or 1.

carry A flag bit in the status register of the central processor used to indicate an operation overflow by the arithmetic logic unit. In MPUs, the carry is also used during shifts.

carry look-ahead A circuit which predicts the final carry from "Propagate" and "Generate" signals supplied by partial adders. It is used to speed up binary addition significantly by eliminating the carry propagation (or ripple) delay.

CAS [*"kaz"*] Column Address Strobe. Used in dynamic memory control for addressing.

cassette A small plastic cartridge which contains two spools of 1/8" magnetic tape and is frequently used in audio recorders. More recently this technology

has been applied to the mass storage requirements of microcomputers and minicomputers. A "digital" cassette is one certified for digital recording, one which meets different standards than those required for audio recording.

CATV CAble TeleVision

CBASIC [*"see-basic"*] A popular BASIC language compiler for 8080, Z80, or 8085 microcomputers. Most BASICs are interpreted rather than compiled.

CBM Commodore Business Machines, a manufacturer of 6502 microprocessor-based computer systems.

CCD Charge-Coupled Device. A technology for storage which uses nothing but MOS capacitors. It is also known as a "bucket brigade" device because of the way it transfers charge from one cell to another in a recirculating fashion.

CDC Control Data Corporation, a manufacturer of large computer systems and peripherals.

cell The repeated unit in a RAM chip, which stores one unit of information and returns that information in response to a particular address signal.

Centronics A manufacturer of printers.

CERDIP [*"sir-dip"*] CERamic Dual-In-line Package

chaining A method of allowing the execution of programs larger than the main memory of a computer by sequentially loading and executing modules of the same program. *See:* overlay.

Challenger A 6502 microprocessor-based personal computer line made by Ohio Scientific, Incorporated.

channel Logical connection from a CPU to an I/O device. Channels may be multiplexed, or have dedicated ports, or even a dedicated channel processor, to optimize the communications throughput.

character generator A circuit which forms the letters or numbers on a display device or printer.

character set The collection of characters available for display or processing on a particular computer or peripheral.

character string A one-dimensional array or sequence of characters. Typically each character is encoded as a byte. Character strings usually either have a length field or are terminated by a special byte., e.g., the zero byte.

checksum A field of one or more bytes appended to a block of n words which contains a truncated binary sum formed from the contents of that block. The sum is used to verify the integrity of data in a ROM or on a tape.

chip A rectangular silicon die cut from a wafer. By extension, every LSI package is commonly called a chip.

chip select Every LSI chip normally has one (or more) chip select(s). The CS line is used to activate one chip among many

which receive similar signals. When selected, the chip examines the rest of its pins, in particular the address bus, which specifies a location/register within the chip. Multiple chip-selects are used to eliminate the need for external decoders, but require extra pins on each chip which uses them.

clear Signal to place a device or a circuit in an initial, known state (usually zero).

CLK Clock

clock The reference timing source in a system. A clock provides regular pulses which trigger or synchronize events. Most microprocessor clocks operate in the range of 1 to 8 MHz. By contrast, real time clocks usually operate at 1, 10, 100 KHz. A system usually requires an MPU clock, a timer clock, plus other clocks for specific I/O devices.

clock frequency The oscillation rate of the clock, usually expressed in Megahertz (MHz).

clock rate See: clock frequency.

close An operation performed on a file, which disassociates it from a particular program.

CML Current Mode Logic

CMOS [*"see-moss"*] Complementary MOS. Technology characterized by a very low power consumption. Used extensively in portable applications (avionics), and for battery-assisted memory systems. CMOS requires a p-channel and an n-channel transistor, and has speed and

density characteristics intermediate between NMOS and PMOS.
CMOS devices may operate at 3V
to 12V. CMOS has ideal noise im-
munity characteristics.

CMR   Common Mode Rejection

CMRR   Common Mode Rejection Ratio. The common mode
gain in operational amplifiers.

coax   [*"ko-ax"*] Coaxial cable. A
transmission line with an inner
conductor and an outer shield
conductor.

COBOL   [*"ko-ball"*] COmmon
Business Oriented Language.
A high-level language with
"English-like" statements de-
signed for business applications.

code   Programming language
statements. *Also:* A symbolic
representation for data.

codec   [*"co-deck"*]   COder-
DECoder. A chip that provides
the essential translation in
analog to digital conversion.

combinational logic   A circuit
consisting of Boolean logic functions with no memory.

comment field   A field within an
instruction, used for explana-
tions and remarks, which are
ignored by the compiler or the
assembler.

compiler   A translation program
which converts high-level instructions into a set of binary
instructions (object code) for
direct processor execution. Any
high-level language requires a
compiler or an interpreter. An
interpreter translates each statement of the program each time
the statement is executed. A
compiler translates the complete
program once, yielding object
code which may then be executed repeatedly. Any change in
the program requires a complete
recompilation. A commonly al-
leged disadvantage of compilers
is that the resulting object code
is often longer or slower than the
code generated by a good programmer in assembly language.
Compare with: assembler, interpreter, translator.

complementing   The action of
changing each 1 to a 0, and each 0
to a 1.

computer   A general purpose
computing system incorporating
a CPU, memory, I/O facilities,
power supply, and cabinet. In a
traditional "mainframe" computer, the CPU alone requires one
or more boards.

computer system   The complete assembly, hardware and
software, with CPU, memory, and
I/O, plus any devices or peripherals required for the application intended.

console   The terminal that has
the most control in a system. For
a microcomputer, the front panel
may be the console, or it may be a
TTY or other device.

constant   An explicit, as opposed to symbolic, value in a program instruction or statement.
Any item whose value is fixed
throughout a program.

control bus   The set of control
lines (10 to 100) in a computer system. Its function is to carry the
necessary synchronization and
control information throughout

the system. Examples of signals carried on these lines are Read, Write ("orders"), Interrupt, Hold, Acknowledge ("sync signals").

control characters   Characters having specific system-dependent meanings.

controller   A circuit board or boards which interfaces a peripheral to the computer, usually having sophisticated circuitry to relieve the processor of device control responsibilities.

control unit   The module in charge of fetching and decoding instructions. The CU requires an Instruction Register, and a Program Counter. It generates control signals, and manages the Control Bus.

conversational   Describes systems in which the computer may respond after each user statement or input. Interactive interpreters provide a conversational high-level language facility.

core   A small magnetic torus of ferrite used to store a bit of information. Cores can be strung on wires so that memory organizations of 32K 18-bit words can be packed into space with dimensions ½" x 6" x 6". The advantages of core are that it is non-volatile, and the oldest main storage technology.

counter   See: binary counter.

CP/M   Control Program for Microcomputers. A popular single-user operating system for 8080, Z80, and 8085-based microcomputers created by Digital Research.

cps   Characters Per Second. Also:

Cycles Per Second, but hertz (Hz) is preferred.

CPU   Central Processing Unit. The computer module in charge of fetching, decoding and executing instructions. It contains a control unit, an ALU, and other related facilities such as registers, clocks, or drivers.

CR   Carriage Return, in ASCII $0D_{16}$. Also: Command Register. Also: Card Reader.

crash   A situation where the system becomes inoperative due to a hardware or software malfunction. A head crash in a disk system refers to the accidental impact of the read/write head on the disk surface.

CRC   Cyclic Redundancy Check. A binary polynomial which is used to check information on blocks of data. When used with an LRC, single-bit errors can be corrected, and 2-bit errors detected. See: LRC.

CROM   ["kromm"] Control Read Only Memory

cross-program   A program for execution on computer A which is created and/or maintained on computer B. An 8080 cross-assembler may reside on a PDP-11, and generate code for the 8080.

crosstalk   Interference between two signals

CRT   Cathode Ray Tube. The television tube used to display pictures or characters, and thus, by extension, a computer terminal which uses a CRT.

CRTC   CRT Controller

crystal   A quartz crystal whose piezoelectric vibrational modes provide a highly accurate frequency for clock timing.

CS   Chip Select

CTS   Clear To Send (RS-232C standard). A control line for the terminal from the modem indicating the carrier is present and data may be sent. See: RS-232C, DSR, DTR.

CU   Control Unit

current loop   A means of communicating data via presence or absence of current on a two-wire cable. Usually associated with 110-baud TTYs.

cursor   A special symbol appearing on video displays which indicates the position of the next character to be inserted or deleted.

custom IC   An integrated circuit manufactured to a customer's specifications. The high development cost restricts custom ICs to large-volume applications (e.g., appliances) or to volume-constrained ones (e.g., military, avionics).

CUTS   Cassette User Tape System

CW   Control Word

cycle-stealing   A method by which another processor, or other type of device, gains access to a microprocessor bus. Rather than granting the cycle to the CPU for fetching, decoding, or executing its instructions, the bus is given to the "cycle stealing" device for its own use for one cycle.

cycle time   Total time required by a device (usually memory) to complete its internal cycle, and become available for use again. Typically, the access time will be shorter than the cycle time.

D   Data line. Also: The hexadecimal symbol for the decimal number 13:
$$D_{16} = 13_{10} = 15_8 = 1101_2.$$

D/A   ["D to A"] Digital to Analog. Conversion from the digital representation used in computers to the analog signals used to drive speakers, motors, etc. Allows computers to act on the external world. See: A/D.

DAA   Data Access Arrangement

DAC   Digital to Analog Converter

daisy chain   A method for prioritizing interrupts. Each unit capable of requesting an interrupt can either pass on the processor acknowledge or block it. In this way the unit electrically closest to the processor has the highest priority.

daisy-wheel printer   An impact printer which uses a wheel having radial spokes bearing type to produce letter-quality output.

DAS   Data Acquisition System

data acquisition   The collection of data from external sensors, usually in analog form.

data base   A systematic organization of data files for central access, retrieval and update.

data bus   The set of lines carrying data. In a standard 8-bit MPU, the data bus is bidirectional, tristate, and has 8 lines. All system components are normally connected to the data bus. In the 8080, the data lines are multiplexed to carry status information, requiring an 8228/8238 "system controller." In the 8085, the data bus is multiplexed with address lines, requiring external demultiplexers.

data file A named collection of information usually stored on magnetic media.

data link escape An escape character used to introduce control information in a data stream, such as ACK. *See:* DLE.

data separator A circuit in disk controllers designed to separate the data from the carrier in the signals read from the disk surface.

data set Modem. *Also:* a group of data elements that are related.

data tablet (or graphics tablet) A graphic input peripheral which digitizes the position of a stylus on a special sensory surface.

data-transfer rate The rate of transfer of data from one place to another, such as from disk to memory or from memory to memory.

data types A specific interpretation applied to binary data, such as integer, real, character, etc.

DAV Data AVailable. One of the 5 status bits of a standard UART. It becomes true when a character has been received. *See:* PE, OR, TBMT.

DBMS Data Base Management System. A program providing a general mechanism for systematic storage and retrieval of data from a data base.

D-bus Internal destination bus in a CPU, from the ALU to the registers.

dc Direct Current

DCE Data Communications Equipment. Equipment used to interface with a data communications network. Generally, a modem. *Contrast with:* DTE.

DCM Data Communication Multiplexor

DC motor A type of motor designed to operate with a direct current power source, often used in variable speed applications.

DCO Digitally Controlled Oscillator

DDCMP DEC's Data Link Control

DDT A DEC software debugging program.

deadlock A situation in which two processes wait indefinitely for each other.

debouncing Eliminating the rapid signal fluctuations which characteristically accompany a change of state in mechanical switches. Mechanical springs bounce repeatedly until the contact is finally closed or opened. Typical debounce time is 5 to 10 ms for stable contact. Debouncing may be performed by hardware (latch) or software (delay).

debugger An essential program designed to facilitate software debugging. At a minimum, it provides breakpoints, dump facilities, register and memory examine/modify, preferably in symbolic form. One of the best known debuggers is DDT (from DEC).

debugging Eliminating the bugs in a system, i.e., troubleshooting and correcting mistakes or errors.

DEC [*"deck"*] Digital Equipment Corporation, manufacturers of the PDP family of computers. The LSI-11 is their best known microcomputer.

decade counter A counter advancing in increments of ten.

decode (cycle) The second cycle of the fetch-decode-execute sequence of instruction execution. The instruction, contained in the IR, is decoded into a set, or a sequence, of control signals to all the required elements of the system, such as register gates, ALU functions, or external devices.

decoder A logical unit which decodes two, three, four or more bits into mutually exclusive outputs. A 3-bit decoder will have $2^3 = 8$ outputs because a 3-bit number can have 8 possible values.

dedicated register A register exclusively used to contain a specific item.

default parameters The parameter values supplied by a computer system when no explicit values are provided by a program or a programmer.

DEL [*"dell"*] DELete character in ASCII, a $7F_{16}$.

demand paging A dynamic memory management technique which loads disk-resident pages into main memory in response to "page faults," i.e., references by programs already in memory to data or instructions that are contained in those pages.

demultiplexer A logical circuit which can route digital signals from one source to various destinations. The unit distributes information to many different points in the system.

DESC Defense Electronics Supply Center. Controls procurement policies and monitors quality for military electronics contracts.

descriptor A binary code attached to an internal item and used to denote its nature, such as syntactic type, or data type.

descenders The portions of printed or displayed characters that extend below the baseline.

development system A computer system with the facilities required for efficient hardware and software application development for a given microprocessor. Such a system typically includes a microcomputer box, CRT display (or TTY), printer, mass-storage (usually dual floppies), PROM programmer, and in-circuit emulator.

development tools Hardware and software aids used in developing programs and/or electronic systems.

D flip-flop A flip-flop with a delayed reaction. The output is conditioned by previous input.

DFR Double Frequency Recording

Diablo A Xerox-owned company which manufactures computer peripherals and computer systems, best known as a supplier of daisy-wheel printers.

diagnostics A set of routines used to diagnose system malfunctions.

die/dice The circuit elements built on small rectangles of silicon on a wafer. Each wafer has several dozen to more than a hundred rectangles—dice. Once mounted in a package, they are referred to as chips.

digital Having discrete states. Digital logic may currently have anywhere from two to sixteen states. Most logic is binary logic, and has two states, on or off.

Digital Analyzers; Logic, Timing Troubleshooting tools which allow the user to identify timing or logic problems.

digilizer A device which converts analog information into its digital equivalent. Often used for devices deriving input from a plotting surface and providing coordinates as output.

diode A device which allows the current to flow in only one direction.

DIP ["dip"] Dual In line Package. A standard IC package with two rows of pins at 0.1" intervals.

DIP switches A collection of small switches on a DIP, used to select options on circuit boards without having to modify the hardware.

direct addressing (short addressing) An addressing technique used for short instructions where the address field is limited to 8 rather than 16 bits.

directory The table of contents of a file system designed to allow convenient access to specific files.

disk Any flat, circular magnetic storage medium which is continuously rotated while in use.

disk controller card A printed-circuit board which interfaces disk storage hardware to the CPU of a computer.

diskette Floppy disk. A flat circle of mylar substrate coated with a magnetic oxide, rotating inside a special jacket which continuously cleans the surface.

disk file A file residing on a disk, or sometimes, the complete disk drive.

display A computer output device designed to temporarily display graphic and/or alphanumeric information, such as a CRT or a seven-segment LED.

DLC Data Link Control

DLE Data Link Escape

DMA Direct Memory Access. The method used to provide high-speed data transfers between a peripheral and the main memory. Data is exchanged at maximum memory speed. Several means for accessing the memory are possible. Disconnecting the MPU from the buses is accomplished by a HOLD signal, and signal, and requires tristate data and address buses. DMA is performed under the control of a DMAC.

DMAC Direct Memory Access Controller. A device, now available as a single chip, used to automate DMA transfers. A DMAC is a specialized block-transfer processor which takes bus control away from the MPU and transfers one or more memory words. A typical DMAC can connect to 4 or 8 devices.

DMM Digital Multi-Meter

DMOS [*"dee-moss"*] Double-diffused MOS

DOD Department of Defense

DO-loop A construct of a high-level language (e.g., FORTRAN) in which a segment of a program is executed repeatedly while or until a certain condition is fulfilled.

DOS [*sometimes "doss"*] Disk Operating System. An operating system whose main secondary storage medium is disk. It typically supplies facilities such as symbolic files, automatic space allocation, and sometimes dynamic memory allocation.

dot matrix A method of forming characters by using many small dots. Usually patterns are 5 by 7, or 7 by 9, though for very high quality characters, patterns of 11 by 13 dots or more are required.

double density The techniques used to double bit density on a magnetic storage medium, such as MFM, M2FM.

double precision arithmetic Arithmetic in which the precision is doubled by using twice as many bits to represent numbers.

double-sided disk A type of disk with both surfaces (sides) available for the storage of data.

DP Data Processing

DPDT Double Pole Double Throw

DPM Digital Panel Meter

DPSK Digital Phase Shift Keying. Encoding digital data into phase differences on a carrier. *See:* phase.

DPST Double Pole Single Throw

drive (device) A mechanical plus electrical/electronic facility required to issue basic commands to a device such as a tape transport or a floppy disk. It may include several motors for rotation, head positioning, etc., and position sensors, control circuits, lights and switches.

driver An amplifier circuit required to reshape signals on a bus when more than one TTL load is present.

drum Rotating magnetic memory using the surface of a cylinder.

DS Data Strobe. Enters data into holding register.

DSR Data-Set Ready (RS-232C standard). A line on the modem telling the data terminal that the received carrier is OK. *See:* RS-232C, DSR, CTS.

DTE Data Terminal Equipment. Equipment which absorbs or originates data, as opposed to Data Communications Equipment, which merely transmits data.

DTL   Diode Transistor Logic

DTR   Data Terminal Ready (RS-232C standard). A line on the terminal telling the modem that it is ready to send data. *See:* RS-232C, DSR, CTS.

dual intensity   A term used to describe printers or display devices which can reproduce symbols in regular and bold-faced formats.

dual-port memory   Memory equipped with dual data and address connections, plus a binary priority circuit. It is used mostly for simple communication between multiple processors and is available in single-chip form for small memory sizes.

dual processors   Used to describe a computer having two CPUs for purposes of redundancy or increasing throughput.

dumb terminal   A low-cost data terminal, usually a CRT, which lacks complicated features such as editing keys or local processing.

dummy variable   A symbol inserted at definition time, which will be replaced later by the actual variable.

dump   An operation in which the contents of one memory level are recorded to another one, e.g., internal registers may be dumped to memory. Memory can be dumped to disk or to a printer.

duplex   Bidirectional communication method which allows simultaneous data transfers in both directions. It may use separate lines, or it may multiplex a single line.

DUT   Device Under Test

dyadic   Describes an operation having two operands, such as addition or multiplication but not negation.

dynamic   Circuitry which stores information as charges on MOS capacitors.

dynamic memory   MOS RAM memory using dynamic circuits. Each bit is stored as a charge on a single MOS transistor. This results in very high density (only one transistor per bit); however, the charge leaks. A typical dynamic memory must be refreshed every 2 ms., by rewriting its entire contents. In practice, this does not slow down the system, but requires additional memory refresh logic. Dynamic memory chips are less expensive than static ones, and are generally preferred for memory sizes over 16K.

dynamic memory allocation   The time-varying allocation of a limited main memory among competing processes according to some system-dependent strategy.

E   Enable. *Also:* The hexadecimal symbol for the decimal number 14:

$$E_{16} = 14_{10} = 16_8 = 1110_2.$$

EA   Electronic Arrays. Manufacturer of semiconductor memories.

EBCDIC   [*"ep-si-dick"*] Extended Binary Coded Decimal Interchange Code. The 8-bit code used by IBM to encode their character set. Based on the original punched card code, it encodes essentially the same characters as ASCII, but in a different numerical order.

echo   A character received from the keyboard is fed back to the printer or CRT for display.

E-beams   Electron beams

ECL   Emitter-Coupled Logic

ECM   Electronic Counter Measures

editor   A program designed to facilitate the entry and maintenance of text in a computer system. Typical facilities include: insert word/line, append, search for "string," substitute (from...to...).

EDP   Electronic Data Processing

EFL   Emitter-Follower Logic

EIA   Electronic Industries Association

EIA-RS-232C   The serial data transmission interface standard for asynchronous communications. Data are sent in 10- or 11-bit serial bundles. The first bit is called the start bit because it signals the beginning of the data. The data bits follow, from least to most significant. After the last data bit comes the stop bit.

electron   The elementary particle circling around the nucleus of an atom. By convention, an electron is one negative charge. The flow of electrons is an electrical current.

electron-beam   A collimated beam of electrons used in IC manufacture and CRT display systems.

ELINT   ELectronic INTelligence

EMI   Electro-Magnetic Interference. Interference caused by electrical fields due to capacitive coupling, or magnetic fields due to mutual inductance, or electromagnetic fields (radio waves).

emulation   Simulation in real time. Computer A emulates computer B by executing an emulator in such a way as to behave like computer B (i.e., it interprets the same instruction set).

END   Statement denoting the end of a program.

ENQ   ENQuiry control character

environment   The state of all registers, memory locations, and other operative conditions in a system.

EOB   End Of Block

EOC   End Of Character. *Also:* End Of Conversion (on an ADC).

EOF   End Of File

EOR   Exclusive OR, (XOR). *Also:* Electro-Optical Reconnaissance.

EOT   End Of Transmission

EPROM   [*"ee-prom"*] Erasable (user-) Programmable Read-Only Memory. A PROM which can be reused several times. Typically refers to an ultraviolet-erasable PROM which can be erased by exposing it for several minutes to hard ultraviolet light. It is then reprogrammed with a special PROM programmer, and will retain its contents for several years. A UV-type EPROM is recognized by its quartz window over the chip. Other EPROMs may be electrically erasable.

error correcting code A code using extra bits which will automatically detect and correct single- or multiple-bit errors.

error correction Describes methods used to correct erroneous data produced by defective or unreliable data storage and transmission systems.

ESC ESCape. A non-printed character that causes the terminal and/or host to interpret subsequent characters differently. Escape codes are used for indicating a sequence of control messages in ASCII.

ETB End of Transmission Block

Ethernet A standard for an inter-computer communications network designed by Xerox Corporation.

ETX End of TeXt

EUROMICRO European Association for Microprocessing and Microprogramming

even parity A parity bit added to a word so that the total number of 1s is even. *See:* parity. *Compare with:* odd parity.

EW Electronic Warfare

excess-3 code A variation of BCD where codes 3 through 12 are used.

execute (cycle) The third of three cycles for program instruction execution. During this time, the actual operation is performed. *See:* fetch (cycle), decode (cycle).

execution time The time required for the execution of an instruction, including fetch-decode-execute.

exerciser A test system or program designed to detect malfunctions in a memory, disk, or tape device prior to use.

expansion board A printed-circuit board which accommodates extra components or cards for the purpose of expanding a computer.

extended arithmetic Usually refers to double-precision floating point operations, and sometimes, to expanded capabilities, such as built-in transcendental functions.

F Flag. *Also:* Finish in BNPF code. *Also:* The hexadecimal symbol for decimal 15—the highest hexadecimal digit:
$$F_{16} = 15_{10} = 17_8 = 1111_2.$$

F-8 Fairchild's 8-bit microprocessor.

Fairchild The oldest semiconductor manufacturer in Silicon Valley.

FAMOS Floating gate Avalanche MOS

fan-fold paper Continuous sheets of paper joined along perforations and folded in a zigzag fashion. Often used with printers because it can be continuously fed and folded without continuous operator assistance.

fan-in An electrical load presented to an output by an input.

fan-out   An electrical load that an output is capable of driving, usually expressed as the number of inputs that can be driven from a given output signal.

farad   A unit of electrical capacitance. A 1 volt per second change in voltage across a 1 farad capacitor will require 1 ampere of current flow.

fast Fourier transform   Application of the Cooley-Tukey algorithm to Fourier transforms. This technique for computing Fourier transforms is ideally suited to computers with respect to time and storage requirements.

fatal error   An unexpected condition occurring during the execution of a program which precludes further running of the program.

fault-tolerant   A program or system capable of correct operation even when some of its components have failed.

FCB   File Control Block. A CP/M-related term describing the block of information set up in main memory. The FCB contains temporary information about an open file.

FCC   Federal Communications Commission

FD   Floppy Disk

FDC   Floppy Disk Controller

FDM   Frequency Division Multiplexing

FE   Framing Error. One of the 5 status bits of a standard UART. It becomes true if the incoming character has no valid stop bit. *See:* PE, OR, DAV, TBMT.

feedback   Monitoring one or more outputs to be used as inputs in a control loop.

FET   [*"fett"*] Field-Effect Transistor

fetch (cycle)   The first cycle in the fetch-decode-execute sequence of instruction execution. During the fetch cycle, the contents of the program counter are placed on the address bus, a Read signal is generated, and PC is incremented. The data word coming from the memory, i.e., the instruction which has been fetched, will be gated into the Instruction Register of the Control Unit.

fetch-ahead   *See:* look-ahead.

FF   Flip-Flop. *Also:* Form Feed. A control character often used with printers, which advances the paper so that the top of the next sheet of paper or the next form is in position for printing.

FFFA   *See:* low byte.

FFFB   *See:* high byte.

FFFF   The hexadecimal representation of the maximum address value on 8-bit microcomputers: $FFFF_{16} = 65535_{10} = 177777_8 = 1111111111111111_2$

FFT   Fast Fourier Transform

field   A logical zone within an instruction, such as opcode, address, or comment.

FIFO   [*"fife-oh"*] First-In-First-Out structure. Data is deposited at one end, and removed from the other. A FIFO is used as a buffer to connect two devices operating asynchronously at different speeds. Each device is connected to one end of the FIFO.

file A logical body of information, with an identifying name, and considered as a unit by a user. A file may be physically divided into records, blocks, or other units as required by the memory device.

File Management System
A collection of programs designed to format and manage user files in a transparent way. The system allows symbolic names and attributes, and manages the physical allocation of storage.

firmware A program stored in a ROM, i.e., software on a hardware support. Historically, firmware was used only for microprograms, but with the advent of microprocessors, many kinds of programs reside in ROM, and firmware designates any ROM-implemented program.

fixed-head disk A disk system with a dedicated head fixed over each track. By eliminating the head positioning delay, it provides very high speed access but at high cost.

fixed-point (representation)
Integer representation where the decimal point is assumed to be in a fixed position. *Contrast with:* floating point (representation).

flag A status indicator associated with a special condition. A flag is normally stored in a flip flop or in a register. Typically, every microprocessor provides at least the following status flags:

carry, zero, sign, overflow, and half-carry.

flip-flop A circuit used to store (as long as power is available) one bit of information permanently. An FF is bistable, with two stable states (0 and 1). Registers are typically assembled out of flip-flops.

flippy Another name for a mini-floppy.

floating gate A technique used for UV-erasable EPROMs, in which a silicon gate is isolated inside the silicon dioxide.

floating-point package A set of software routines necessary to perform floating-point arithmetic: add, subtract, multiply, normalize. To assure precision, the design of an FPP requires careful analysis of error propagation phenomena, and is a complex task.

floating-point (representation)
The integer representation of decimal numbers within a fixed length format, such as 24 or 32 bits. The number N is normalized and encoded as a mantissa field M and an exponent field E: $N = M \times e^E$ where $0.1 \leqslant |M| < 1$. The name is derived from the fact that the representation remains fixed as the decimal point floats, i.e., the changes in magnitude are reflected by adjustment of the exponent field with renormalization of the mantissa field. The precision of the representation is limited by the number of bits allocated to the mantissa field. *Contrast with:* fixed-point (representation).

floppy disk   A mass-storage device using a flexible (floppy) mylar disk (diskette) to record information. The diskette is permanently sealed in a square plastic jacket lined with a soft material which cleans the diskette as it rotates. A cut-out slot provides access to the moving head which must actually come in contact with the diskette surface in order to read or write. Other holes in the jacket provide access to sector index holes in the diskette itself.

floppy mini   A smaller floppy that is 5-1/4″ square compared to 8″ for the standard floppy.

flowchart   A symbolic representation of a program sequence. Boxes represent orders or computations. Diamonds represent tests and decisions (branches). A flowchart is a recommended step between algorithm specification and program writing. It greatly facilitates understanding and debugging the program by breaking it into logical, sequential steps.

flyback   The time period during which the spot on a CRT comes back to the beginning of a frame.

FMS   File Management System

foreground program   In a multiprogramming environment, a higher priority program. *Also:* a program in charge of interfacing with a user or a process. *See:* background program.

formatter   A circuit or program which writes the file marks, track marks, address marks, preambles, postambles and check characters for floppy disks, disks, or tape drives.

Formulator   A development system for the F-8 microprocessor.

Forth   A programming language system characterized by threaded code and postfix, or reverse Polish, notation. It might therefore be thought of as Polish BASIC.

FORTRAN   [*"for-tran"*] FORmula TRANslator. An early high-level language devised for numerical computations. Although somewhat complex and obsolete, it is still one of the most used programming languages in scientific environments. It requires a compiler. (By contrast, BASIC, derived from FORTRAN, can be interpreted.)

Fourier transform   The mathematical analysis of a complex wave-form into harmonics.

FPGA   Field Programmable Gate Array

FPLA   Field Programmable Logic Array. A PLA which can be programmed by the user. FPLAs are used in particular to implement the control section of bit-slice processors.

FPLS   Field Programmable Logic Sequencer (Signetics).

FPP   Floating Point Package

fragmentation   A situation in which mass memory has been allocated in such a way that it has many unallocated areas (fragments) that are too small to be useful. The remedy for fragmentation is compacting all of the allocated areas into a single area to make the space occupied by fragments available in one large block.

frame   The necessary underlying structure for a record, file, or other data entity. The frame creates an organization within which the data takes its place.

frequency   The number of cycles per second. $F = 1/T$ where T is the period.

front-end processor   The processor in charge of interfacing with a user or a process. The front-end may perform pre-processing translations or file handling, while the main processor performs interpretation, execution or number-crunching.

front panel   A panel with lights and switches designed to facilitate debugging by displaying information, and allowing direct control or access to memory or registers. A front panel requires a specific interface plus a monitor program. Many microcomputers have no front panel, and all debugging is done from a terminal.

FS   File Separator

FSC   Full SCale range

FSK   Frequency Shift Keying. A 0 is given one frequency, and a 1 is given a different frequency. These two tones are then transmitted over telephone or radio links and converted back to logic signals upon reception. *See:* modem.

full duplex   A mode of communication in which data may be transmitted and received simultaneously.

fully decoded selection   A method of selecting memory locations or input/output devices through a full n-bit address (typically n = 16). This requires the use of decoders, but allows full utilization of 64K possible addresses.

fundamental   The frequency under consideration. It is usually a pure sine wave with no distortion.

F/V   Frequency to Voltage Converter

G   Ground. *Also:* Generate signal. The output from an adder designed for connection to a carry lookahead circuit. It also requires a propagate signal.

gain   The output to input amplification ratio.

gap   The space between two records or two blocks of information on a magnetic memory. A gap is usually set to a predetermined value, such as all zeroes. It allows blocks to be rewritten in a slightly expanded or reduced format, due to speed variations of the drive.

garbage collection   A technique for collecting unavailable, unused space in a mass memory and making it available for reuse by any of several schemes.

gate   A single logic function. The NAND, NOR, AND, OR, XOR, and NOT functions are examples of gates.

Gauss   A unit of flux density

(1 Maxwell per square cm.), named after German mathematician Karl F. Gauss.

GCR   Group Coded Recording

GE   General Electric. *Also:* Greater than or Equal to (also represented by $>=$ or $\geqslant$).

GI   General Instruments, a manufacturer.

Gibson Mix   A statistically balanced mix of instructions that is typical of general data processing applications. It is one of many variations used for benchmark testing.

glitch   A pulse or burst of noise. A small pulse of noise is called a snivitz. The word glitch is sometimes reserved for the more annoying types of noise pulses which cause crashes and failures.

global variable   A variable whose name and value are accessible throughout the program. This is opposed to a local variable, accessible only within the block where it is defined.

GND   Ground

GOTO (or GO TO)   A branch instruction in a high-level language.

GP   General Purpose

GPIB   General Purpose Interface Bus. The name used for the IEEE 488-1975 interface bus standard. Also known as ANSI Standard MC 1.1-1975, or the IEC Bus in Europe.

ground   The point of reference in an electrical circuit (not necessarily the physical ground). The ground point is considered to be at nominal zero potential, and all other potentials in the circuit are compared to it.

GT   Greater Than (also represented by $>$).

H   Hexadecimal. Used as a suffix to denote hexadecimal numbers in Intel format. *For example:* 0F3AH. In this notation, hexadecimal numbers beginning with A to F must be prefixed with a leading zero. *Also:* High. The most significant half of a register or a pointer; usually bits 0 to 7 of a 16-bit word.

H-8   An 8080 microprocessor-based hobbyist computer system available from Heathkit.

half-carry   The carry from bit 3 into bit 4 required for adding packed BCD numbers correctly, where two BCD digits reside in one 8-bit byte.

half-duplex   A mode of communication in which data may be transmitted in only one direction at a time.

halt   The state where a computer stops and does nothing.

Hamming code   A 7-bit error-correcting code named after its inventor.

handler   A section of a program used to control or communicate with an external device.

handshaking   A basic communication synchronizing technique using two signals: 1 — ready?; 2 — yes/no acknowledgment. The handshaking procedure is carried out when establishing a connection between two data communication devices prior to any data transfer. For example, an MPU will ask a PIO: is input buffer 1 empty? If yes, it can be reloaded. If no, the MPU must wait.

hard copy Computer output printed on paper

hard disk A disk composed of a magnetic coating applied to a rigid substrate, such as aluminum or ceramic. The term is generally used to contrast with 'soft' (floppy) disks, which are flexible but are slower and have less storage capacity.

hard-sectored Describes a disk in which the recording surface has been divided into sectors using non-alterable methods, such as a ring of holes in the disk itself.

hardware The boards, chips, wires, nuts and bolts, etc.; i.e., the physically existing components of a system.

hard wired The implementation of a function with logic gates, i.e., with hardware rather than software.

harmonic An integer multiple of a fundamental frequency.

harmonic distortion Distortion due to the signal's non-linear characteristics, resulting in output which includes harmonics of a pure sine input.

Hazeltine A manufacturer of video terminals and related equipment.

HDLC Higher Data Link Control

head crash The physical impact of a disk head on the disk resulting in damage to its surface (for hard disks).

heap A section of memory organized as a stack, used by some Pascal compilers to store dynamic (pointer) variables during program execution.

henry A unit of inductance. A rate of change of 1 ampere per second per second in a current passing through an inductance of 1 henry will induce a voltage of 1 volt.

Hertz (Hz) A unit of frequency, named after physicist Heinrich Hertz. An AC line frequency is 50 Hz in Europe and 60 Hz in the U.S. This means the voltage changes polarity 100 or 120 times per second.

hex, hexadecimal The base 16 representation of numbers. The digits 0 through 9 are used, then A to F, to represent decimal numbers from 0 to 15. For example, "FF" represents "11111111" binary. "0A" is "00001010" binary. Hexadecimal is universally used in the microcomputer world, as it encodes one byte in just two symbols. Single-board microcomputers allow hex input through a keyboard, and hex output through LEDs.

high address An address with a high numerical value when viewed as an unsigned integer. The highest address in a 64K memory is $FFFF_{16}$.

high byte (FFFB) Bits 8 through 15 of a 16-bit binary number.

high-level language Any programming language resembling "natural language", with powerful instructions. Examples are FORTRAN, BASIC, APL, ALGOL, COBOL, PL/M. A high-level language (HLL) requires a compiler, or an interpreter.

high-order The most significant part. In a 16-bit word, typically bits 8-15.

high resolution A quality of video graphics display systems or printers capable of reproducing images in great detail to a high degree of accuracy.

highway *See:* bus.

HLL High-Level Language

HMOS [*"H-moss"*] High density MOS.

hobby computer A computer not used for profit (or a tax write-off!).

HOL [*sometimes as in "hol-ly"*] High-Order Language. *See:* high-level language.

Hollerith code The code used on punched cards, named after its inventor.

HP Hewlett-Packard, a manufacturer.

HP-85 A personal computer manufactured by Hewlett-Packard with an integral keyboard, a video display, a printer, and a cartridge tape drive.

HPIB Hewlett-Packard Interface Bus. Another name for the IEEE 488-1975 bus, also known as GPIB.

HSYNC [*"H-sink"*] Horizontal SYNChronization. Refers to the signal in a TV that determines the horizontal position of the image displayed.

HTL High Threshold Logic. It is used in industrial environments.

hybrid A single circuit package that has two or more separate chips inside.

Hz Hertz. Unit of frequency.

I Integrated. *Also:* Index. *Also:* Interrupt. *Also:* Immediate.

I²L [*"eye-squared-ell"*] Integrated Injection Logic

iAPX432 A 32-bit, three-chip microprocessor made by Intel Corporation.

IBM International Business Machines, the world's largest computer manufacturer.

IC Integrated Circuit

ICE [*"ice"*] In-Circuit Emulation (Intel term).

ID Identification

IEEE [*"I-triple-E"*] Institute of Electrical and Electronic Engineers

IEEE 488 See: GPIB.

IEEE 583/CAMAC The industrial hardware/software instrumentation standards developed for the nuclear industry but also used in many industrial applications.

IEEE 696 The IEEE S-100 bus standard.

IF-THEN-ELSE A program statement used in high-level languages. If a certain logical assertion is true, the statement following the THEN is executed. If the assertion is not true, the statement following the ELSE is executed.

immediate addressing A mode where the address of the location

location in memory to be read or written is specified in the instruction itself.

IMP [*"imp"*] An early bit-slice processor from National Semiconductor. *Also:* Interface Message Processor in the ARPA network.

impact printer   Any mechanical printing device which forms characters by striking ribbon onto paper.

in-circuit emulation   A hardware/software facility for realtime I/O debugging. The actual MPU is replaced by a connector (typically 40 pin) whose signals are generated by an emulation program. The emulated MPU can be stopped, and its registers examined or modified. I/O devices can be controlled from the development system's console. Programs can reside in (simulated) RAM memory, or actual ROMs/PROMs.

incremental compiler   A compiler capable of compiling additional statements in a program without completely recompiling the program.

incrementer   A hardware component which automatically adds one.

indexed addressing   A mode in which the actual effective address is obtained by adding a displacement to a base address. In most microprocessors, the displacement is in an index register (8 bits), and the base address in a field in the instruction.

index hole   A hole punched in a floppy disk to indicate the beginning of the first sector.

index register   A register whose contents can be added automatically to an address field contained in an instruction, in order to obtain the effective address when an indexed addressing mode is specified.

indirect addressing   A mode where the address of the location in memory to be read or written is contained in a register or in another place in memory.

information system   A computer system oriented towards data storage and retrieval, often using a DBMS.

initialization   Starting the processor in a known state. *See:* clear, reset.

ink-jet printer   A technology where characters are printed by electrostatically aiming a jet of ink onto the paper.

input/output   Describes lines or devices used to convey information between the computer system and the outside world.

instruction   A single order within a program. This order will be fetched from memory, decoded, and executed by the CPU. Instructions may be arithmetic or logical, and they may operate on registers, memory, or I/O devices. A sequence of instructions is a program.

instruction decoder   The unit in the CPU which converts program instructions in binary code into the necessary control signals for the ALU, registers, and control bus.

instruction set The basic operations that can be performed by a CPU. Necessary instructions are arithmetic, logical, test and branch, and data moving.

INT INTerrupt. Also refers to the interrupt pin on some microprocessor chips.

integer math Describes mathematics software capable of operating only on integer numbers and generating integer results.

integrated circuit A circuit which is fabricated on a single chip of silicon.

Integrated Injection Logic (I^2L) bipolar technology for LSI fabrication, characterized by low power consumption.

Intel INTegrated ELectronics, a major semiconductor manufacturer.

intelligent controller A device controller equipped with local capabilities, such as editing, input validity checking, and complex command decoding.

interactive Refers to a computer system with which the user has a dialog: i.e., with which each entry by the user can cause a response by the system. *See:* batch.

interface The hardware/software required to interconnect a device to a system or one system to another. One-chip hardware interfaces now exist for most peripheral devices.

interlace The technique used in a raster scan display to provide superimposed images. Each line of the second image is between two lines of the previous one. *Also:* sometimes used as a synonym for interleaving.

interleaving Assigning sequentially addressed entities to nonsequential physical addresses to maximize throughput.

internal timer An internal clock equipped with multiple registers that can monitor the duration of external events, or generate a pulse after a fixed time.

interpreter A translation program used to carry out statements expressed in a high-level language. An interpreter translates each statement and executes it immediately. Instructions can be interactively added or modified in an interpreted program, and execution may be resumed at once without any further action. Interpreted programs are much slower than compiled ones because a statement must be translated each time it is executed. *See:* compiler, translator.

interrupt A signal sent from an I/O device or chip to the MPU to request service. When accepted, the interrupt causes the MPU to save its current state (program counter, internal registers, etc.) and to branch to an appropriate handler. After the interrupt has been handled or the requested service is completed, the saved state is restored and the interrupted program execution resumes. Multiple interrupts must be prioritized.

interrupt handler An I/O routine which services a specific interrupt.

Interrupt vectoring Providing a device ID number, or an actual branching address in response to the interrupt acknowledge signal from the processor. New PICs provide automatic interrupt vectoring for up to eight interrupts.

interval timer An electronic circuit which interrupts the CPU at hardware- or software-specified time intervals, often used for timekeeping in process control.

inverter An electronic circuit whose output is the binary NOT function of its input.

I/O Input/Output

I/O-bound Describes processes in which the rate of input and/or output of data is the factor determining program speed.

I/O port A data channel or connection to external devices used for input and/or output to and from a computer.

I/O processor A special-purpose computer designed to relieve a computer system's primary processor(s) of the time-consuming task of managing input and output operations.

IPL Initialize Program Load. The Initialization routine used in intelligent controllers.

ips [*"ipps"*] Inches Per Second

IR Instruction Register. The register which holds the current instruction being decoded and executed by the CPU control section. *Also:* InfraRed. *Also:* Interna-

tional Rectifier, a manufacturer of semiconductors.

IRQ Interrupt ReQuest signal

ISAM [*"eye-sam"*] Indexed Sequential Access Method (IBM term).

ISIS Intel System Implementation Supervisor. The resident operating system in Intel's 8080 microprocessor-based development systems.

ISO International Standards Organization. The codes authorized by the ISO, and used to represent alphanumeric and special characters.

ISO Standard A standard proposed or adopted by the International Standards Organization, which functions in Europe similarly to ANSI in the U.S. Thus, what is known in the U.S. as the ASCII character set is known in Europe as the ISO character set.

iterative Characterized by repetition.

ITT International Telephone and Telegraph

IX IndeX register

J Jump instruction

JAN [*"jan"*] Joint Army Navy program for standardizing military equipment.

JAWS [*"jaws"*] Jamming And Warning System

JCL Job Control Language

J-K flip-flop A flip-flop whose output is conditioned by the combination of inputs on J-K.

JOLT A microcomputer board

which uses the 6502 microprocessor.

joystick   A stick, normally vertical, which can be tilted in any direction to indicate direction of movement. It is often used to position a cursor on a screen.

jump   An instruction which causes the next instruction executed to be the one at the address specified in the jump. Typically, a jump is conditional: branching will occur only if a specified condition occurs. Otherwise, execution will proceed to the next instruction following the jump instruction.

jumper selectable   A function which is specified by connecting or disconnecting wires (called jumpers) on a circuit card.

justification   Alignment of text against a right or left margin.

K   (Kilo-) Symbol for 10^3. In computer contexts K is usually taken to be 2^{10}, 1024_{10}. A 4K chip is a 4,096 bit chip. A 64K memory is a 65,536 word (or byte) memory.

Kansas City Standard   The standard for cassette tape recording and playback of EIA-RS-232C data. The encoding technique represents a 1 by 8 cycles of 2400 Hz, and a 0 by 4 cycles of 1200 Hz.

Katakana   A set of characters used in Japanese primarily to transcribe foreign (i.e., non-Japanese) words. Obviously much used in Japanese computer-related text.

KB   Kilo-Byte, 1024 bytes.

KCS   Kansas City Standard

keyboard   A group of buttons on a pad used to input information into a computer system.

keypad   A small keyboard, usually a small number of special-purpose keys.

keyword   A characteristic word in a title, abstract, file, or part of a file used to describe it, label it, and/or provide the means for identifying and retrieving it.

kilobaud   One thousand bits per second.

Kilobaud/Microcomputing   A hobby magazine for personal and small computer users.

KIM   A single-board computer using the 6502 microprocessor, made by MOS Technology.

kips   [*"kipps"*] Kilo Instructions Per Second. A unit of machine speed equalling 1,000 operations per second. The MOS LSI microprocessors execute about 500 kips. Larger computers such as the PDP-11/70 execute 3000 kips. *Also:* a famous Berkeley eating place.

kit   A system which is assembled by the user.

kludge   A patch or trick to correct an error locally, as opposed to clean design.

KSAM   Keyed Sequential Access Method

KSR   Keyboard Send Receive. A terminal having only a keyboard and printer, but no means for automatic origination or retention of data. *Contrast with:* ASR.

L   Low

label A symbolic name for an address.

landing The inside connection that leads to the pins on the package.

large scale integration (LSI) The technology by which thousands of semiconductor devices are fabricated on a single silicon chip. *See:* chip, MOS, wafer.

latch A hardware device which senses information and holds it until reset.

LCD Liquid Crystal Display

LE Less than or Equal to (also represented by $<=$ or $\leqslant$).

learning curve The improvement profile observed in the performance of any operation as the operator gains in experience.

least significant bit The binary digit having a weight of 2^0 or 1.

LED [*sometimes "led"*] Light Emitting Diode

letter quality Describes printers which produce high-quality output, usually using impact methods with die-cast type.

Level II BASIC An implementation of Microsoft BASIC for the TRS-80 computer system from Radio Shack.

levels Voltage values conventionally used to encode discrete signals in digital systems.

LF Line Feed

LI Left In. The left input to a shifter.

librarian A program that manages a library of files.

library A collection of programs.

LIFO Last-In-First-Out. A device or data structure in which the most recent item stored is the first item available for retrieval, as in a stack.

light emitting diode A diode which emits light when a current flows through it. LEDs emit infrared, red, orange, yellow, or green light.

light pen A device which, when placed against a CRT screen, can be tracked by the computer. It is used to select data on the CRT face, and sometimes to trace curves as input to a program.

linear regulator A power supply design in which the voltage is held constant by dissipating 50% of the input voltage times the output current as a margin.

linear selection A method of selecting memory or input/output devices that dedicates one address line per chip selection. This results in overlapping or non-contiguous memory. It is used because it is the cheapest method of selection. *See:* fully decoded selection.

line driver A digital signal amplifier.

line feed A character or command which moves the paper up one line on a printer or the cursor down one line on a CRT.

line printer A high speed printer capable of printing one complete line (80 to 132 characters) at a time.

line surge A sharp change in the AC power line voltage which can damage unprotected computer circuitry.

linker A program which gathers and unites separately written programs or routines for subsequent loading into memory and execution.

linking loader A program that takes a set of program segments and binds them together in one particular memory configuration, adjusting instruction addresses appropriately to match the resulting placement of the segments in memory.

LISP [*"lisp" or "lithp"*] An interpretive LISt Processing language which predominates in the artificial intelligence community.

listing A printed representation of a computer program.

literal A constant within an instruction, representing data.

LO Left Out. The left output from a shifter.

load The action of transferring data from a memory location into a register, or a program from the place where it is stored into the place where it is to execute.

loader An operating system utility program which places programs which are to be run in actual physical memory.

local variable A variable whose scope is limited to a particular block of code, function, procedure, subroutine or program.

lock A mechanism for controlling multiple accesses to a common device such as a bus or memory.

logic analyzer A test and diagnostic system equipped with an oscilloscope, and capable of displaying bus and other digital states as 0s and 1s, and performing complex test functions as well.

logic state analyzer *See:* analyzer.

logic timing analyzer *See:* analyzer.

look-ahead Internal register queue for instructions.

loop A group of instructions that may be executed more than once.

loop counter A register used to implement high-speed branching for loops, including single instruction loops. A loop counter must be able to be tested and decremented in the same instruction.

low byte (FFFA) Bits 0 through 7 of a 16-bit binary number.

low-end MPU A single-chip microcomputer designed for low-cost applications, generally with some on-board RAM and ROM plus I/O or clock capabilities.

low order The least significant half of a word. Usually bits 0-7 of a 16-bit word.

low pass A filter which transmits low-frequency signals.

low-power Schottky logic A TTL-compatible logic family offering low power consumption and high switching speed.

LP Line Printer

lpm Lines Per Minute

lps Lines Per Second

LPS Low-Power Schottky. *See:* low-power Schottky logic.

LRC Longitudinal Redundancy Check. A binary polynomial used to generate check information on blocks of data. *See:* CRC.

LSB Least Significant Bit

LSI Large Scale Integration

LSI-11 Microcomputer made by DEC, emulating the PDP-11.

LSTTL Low-power Schottky Transistor-Transistor Logic. *See:* low-power Schottky logic and TTL.

LT Less Than (also represented by $<$).

M Memory. *Also:* Million. *Also:* Military.

machine Trade jargon used to refer to a computer or a processor.

machine language A set of binary codes representing the memory configurations which can be directly executed by a processor as instructions.

machine-readable Information represented in such a way that it may be read into a computer using electronic and/or mechanical means.

macro assembler An assembler equipped with a facility for defining and expanding macro instructions.

macro instruction An instruction which stands for a predefined sequence of other instructions, called the 'body' of the macro. Whenever a macro instruction is encountered in

program text, it is 'expanded', i.e., replaced by its body.

mail-box A file or memory area in which messages for a particular destination are placed.

mainframe The main portion of the computer, including the CPU, memory, and peripheral interfaces. *Also:* A large computer.

main storage High-speed, directly addressable memory for program and data, typically ROM + RAM.

mapping PROM A PROM in charge of converting an opcode into a microprogram starting address.

MAR Memory Address Register

mark Binary 1, realized in the RS-232C standard as a positive voltage; in a current loop as a 20 milliampere current; and in modems as the higher frequency of the pair. *See:* space.

mask (1) In computer system logic: a pattern of bits in a memory location or register which is used to select, ignore, set or clear other bits or bit patterns. Mask operations frequently make use of the logical instructions AND, OR and XOR. (2) In IC technology: a pattern, usually etched on glass, used to define areas of the chip on the wafer. Masks are used for the diffusion, oxidation, and metallization steps.

maskable interrupts Interrupt signals which are ignored by the CPU on software command.

masked ROM Regular ROM whose contents are produced during its manufacture by the usual masking process. This is in contrast to a PROM whose contents are "programmed" after its manufacture by means of a PROM programming device.

mass storage   The secondary, slower memory used for storing large files or large numbers of small files. Typical mass storage devices for microcomputer systems are moving-head disks, floppy disks, or cassette tapes.

master processor   The main processor in a master/slave configuration.

matrix character   A character displayed or printed from a matrix of dots, such as on a CRT screen.

maxwell   Unit of magnetic flux.

MBASIC   ["M-basic"] Microsoft BASIC.

MDR   Memory Data Register

MDS   Microprocessor Development System. A microcomputer equipped with hardware and software facilities to carry out program development and hardware debugging for microprocessor systems. This usage was common in the 1970s, but the initials have been a registered trademark of Mohawk Data Sciences Corp. since the 1960s, and any other usage violates their trademark.

medium scale integration (MSI)   The technology by which 10 to 100 gates are fabricated on a single silicon chip. See: large scale integration.

megabyte   1024 x 1024 bytes, or 1024K. 8 million bits.

Memorex   A manufacturer of magnetic media and storage systems.

memory   A storage area for binary data and programs. Also: Any device which will store information. In a computer, memory is divided into fast electronic memory integral to the computer, and external, slower memory such as disk drives and tape drives, using magnetic recording methods.

memory allocation   The technique by which memory is allocated to processes or devices.

memory array   Memory cells arranged in a rectangular geometric pattern on a chip, and organized in rows and columns.

memory bank   A block of memory locations responding to contiguous addresses. See: bank select.

memory management   A combination of hardware and software systems which allocate memory to programs and data blocks in a multiprogramming system.

memory map   A drawing or table showing the allocation of system memory areas to devices, programs, or functions. Also: The hardware for transforming virtual addresses into physical addresses in a time-sharing or multiprocessing system.

memory-mapped I/O   An addressing technique in which I/O devices are addressed as memory locations.

memory-mapped video   A method of CRT information and graphics display where each character or pixel location on the screen corresponds to a unique memory location which the CPU may access.

memory protection A mechanism used to prevent accidental writing into a memory location or area.

menu A set of options or choices displayed by a program from which the user may choose.

merge To combine two ordered files of information items in such a way as to maintain the ordering of the items of the original files in the resulting file.

MFM Modified Frequency Modulation

M²FM Modified Double Frequency Modulation

MHz MegaHertz. 1 MegaHertz = 10^6 cycles per second.

micro A numerical prefix meaning 10^{-6}.

microcomputer A complete small system, including microprocessor CPU, memory, I/O interfaces and power supply.

microprocessor An LSI implementation of a complete processor (ALU + Control Unit) on a single chip. It is the CPU of the microcomputer.

microprogram A special program which sequences the control unit of a processor. It implements sequential instruction fetch, plus decoding and execution by providing the appropriate signals to the required gates. Most MPUs are internally microprogrammed by the manufacturer, but cannot be microprogrammed by the

user. Bit-slices are user-microprogrammable.

mil [*"mill"*] (1) .001 inch or dollar. (2) Abbreviation for military as in "mil spec" for military specification.

military temperature range The range from $-55°$ to $+125°C$.

MIL-STD-883 The basic military standard for reliable semiconductors. Three classes are defined: A (aerospace), B (avionics), and C (ground).

mini-disk A floppy disk having a protective jacket 5.25 inches square. *Also:* the disk drive used to store data on a mini-disk.

minus flag A flag bit in the status register of the CPU. Used to indicate a negative result from an arithmetic operation. In twos-complement representation, a negative result occurs when the high order bit of the number is 1.

MMI Monolithic Memories, Inc., a semiconductor manufacturer.

mnemonic A symbolic representation, generally of an opcode. Examples are ADD, SUB, and MPY.

MNOS [*"em-noss"*] Metal Nitride Oxide Semiconductor. The technology used for EAROMs (electrically alterable ROMs), not to be confused with NMOS.

modem MOdulator-DEModulator. A device used to interface a digital device to a telephone line, it encodes and decodes serial bits into frequencies.

modified frequency modulation An encoding technique

used on high-performance disk drives, such as the IBM 3330, to double the bit density.

monitor A program or collection of programs implementing the fundamental set of commands required to operate a computer system. The monitor must manage physical resources, such as a front-panel or input keyboard.

Moore's Curve A curve showing the actual doubling of component density every year, and first proposed in public by Dr. Gordon Moore, one of Intel's founders.

MOS [*sometimes "moss"*] Metal-Oxide Semiconductor. A technology used for fabricating high-density ICs, so named for the three successive layers of materials used. Most LSI devices, such as microprocessors, are based on MOS technology.

MOSFET [*"moss-fet"*] Metal-Oxide Semiconductor Field Effect Transistor

most-significant bit The bit in the left-most position.

motherboard The main board equipped with female connectors in which all functional boards are inserted. It carries the system buses. Also called a backplane.

moving head disk An economical type of disk drive using a single head to access all the tracks.

MP/M Multiprogramming Control Program for Microprocessors. A multi-programming, multi-terminal version of the CP/M operating system from Digital Research.

MPU MicroProcessor Unit

MPY MultiPlY

MR Memory Read

ms MilliSecond. 1 millisecond $= 10^{-3}$ seconds.

MSB Most Significant Bit

MSI Medium Scale Integration

MTBF Mean Time Between Failures

MTTR Mean Time To Repair

multibus A bus standard designed and supported by Intel for a multiple-processor system.

multimicroprocessor system A configuration with several interconnected MPUs. Interconnections may be through memory, PIO, or buses.

multiplex Sharing one resource among several users. For example, in communications, the concurrent transmission of more than one information stream on a single channel.

multiplexer The device or technique used to share a resource, such as a memory or a bus.

multiprocessing Denotes computer systems with multiple processors.

multiprogramming A method for achieving apparent simultaneous execution of multiple programs by interleaving their execution.

MUX [*"mucks"*] MUltipleXer

MW Memory Write

N The negative of the sign flag. It denotes the sign of a word in twos-complement notation, and usually N is the MSB.

NAK ["*nack*"] Negative AcKnowledge

NAND ["*nand*"] Logical NOT-AND

native code Machine-dependent language, such as an assembly language.

native compiler A compiler which produces code for the processor on which it runs.

NBS National Bureau of Standards

NC No Connection

NDAC Not Data ACcepted (IEEE 488 standard).

NDRO Non-Destructive Read Out

NE Not Equal to (also represented by < > or ≠).

NEC [*sometimes "neck"*] Nippon Electric Corporation

negative logic A logical false state is represented by the normally true state voltage in the system, and the logical true state is represented by the normally false state voltage in the system. For TTL, 0 becomes +2.5 volts or greater, and 1 becomes + 6 volts or less. *See:* positive logic.

NEQ Not EQual to. *See:* NE.

nested (subroutine) A subroutine called or defined within another subroutine.

network A system of interconnected computers, which may take on such configurations as rings, stars, or chains.

nibble Usually 4 bits or half a byte.

NMI Non-Maskable Interrupt. An interrupt at the highest priority which is not affected by an interrupt mask. It is typically used in the event of a power failure.

NMOS ["*en-moss*"] The N-channel MOS, the LSI technology introduced after PMOS. It offers better speed, but less density. It is currently optimum for MPU implementation.

noise Random signals or other interference on a line.

non-destructive read-out Memory in which a read operation does not erase the contents.

NOP, NOOP [*always "no-op"*] NO-OPeration. An instruction used to force a delay of one instruction cycle without changing the status flags or the contents of registers.

NOR Logical NOT-OR

NOT The logical negation operator. Logical complement: the changing of every 0 to a 1 and every 1 to a 0 in a byte, word or other collection of binary data.

Nova One of the classical 16-bit minicomputers (made by Data General). It served as the model for early 16-bit microprocessors such as the Texas Instrument 9900 series and National Semiconductor's IMP and PACE.

n-p-n A transistor with a p-type substrate (in MOS implementation). The base and drain are n, i.e., doped with n-type impurities (excess electrons).

NRFD Not Ready For Data (IEEE 488 standard).

NRZ   Non-Return to Zero. Each state of the medium is either 0 or 1.

NRZ·L   Non Return to Zero-Level

NS   National Semiconductor, a major Silicon Valley manufacturer of a wide variety of chips.

nsec   Nanosecond. 1 nanosecond = 10^{-9} seconds.

null detector   A circuit which detects when no current is flowing or no voltage is present.

null modem   Two RS-232C female connectors wired back to back, so that the output pins of each are connected to the input pins of the other. This device allows two pieces of standard RS-232C data terminal equipment (DTEs), e.g., a CRT and a computer, to be connected to one another directly without any other data communication equipment (DCE), such as a modem.

number crunching   Performing complex numerical operations or arithmetic-intensive computation.

numeric pad   A keyboard for numeric input to a computer.

NVM   Non-Volatile Memory

O   Output. *Also:* Overflow.

OASIS   A time-sharing operating system from Phase One Systems.

object code   The output code produced by a translator program, such as a compiler or assembler. It may be directly executable by the processor when it is loaded (absolute object code),

or it may require a "linkage" phase prior to loading and execution.

O/C   Open Collector

OCR   Optical Character Recognition

octal   A numerical representation system where the digits 0 through 7 are used to encode each of the eight possible sequences of 3 bits from 000 to 111. In microprocessing circles, octal has been essentially superseded by hexadecimal representation, which is more convenient for representing 8-, 16- and 32-bit numbers.

odd parity   A system in which a parity bit is added to a word so that the total number of 1s is odd. *Contrast with:* even parity.

OE   Output Enable

OEM   Original Equipment Manufacturer. A manufacturer who uses computers or components as part of the package of products they sell, as opposed to end users, who buy computers for their own use and not for resale.

off-line   Disconnected from the computer system.

one-chip   A device implemented in a single chip.

ones-complement   A representation system for signed binary integers where the negative of a number is obtained by complementing it. The left-most bit becomes a sign bit, with 0 for plus and 1 for minus.

on-line Directly connected to the computer system.

opamp OPerational AMPlifier

opcode OPeration CODE

open To associate a file with a running program.

operand An object on which or with which an operation is performed. *See:* operator.

operating system The software required to manage the hardware and logical resources of a system, including device handling, process scheduling and file management.

operation A specified, defined action, such as a machine-language instruction.

operation code (opcode) The segment of the machine language or assembly language instruction specifying the operation to be performed. The other instruction segments specify the operands: the registers, storage addresses, or input/output ports. By extension, in the microprocessor world, the opcode includes the first 6 bits.

operator A symbol in a programming language representing an operation to be performed on one or more operands, e.g., "+" (add), or "×" (multiply).

optimization Altering hardware or software to maximize performance.

opto-coupler The same as opto-isolator. *See:* opto-isolator.

opto-isolator A device which modulates data on light beams so that the data processing system can remain optically coupled, but electrically isolated from the source of the data.

OR OverRun. One of the 5 status bits of a standard UART. It goes to 1 if a new character is written over an old one (DAV not reset). *See:* PE, FE, DAV, TBMT.

OS Operating System

OV OVerflow

overflow A bit of the status register used to indicate whether or not twos-complement overflow has occurred. It denotes an overflow from bit 6 into bit 7 (i.e., the sign bit).

overlay A memory management technique in which different routines use the same memory locations (overlay areas or segments) depending on which is needed at the time. This technique will work well as long as no two routines from different overlays that are using the same area are needed at the same time.

Overrun Error An error in which the previous character in a register has not been completely read by the MPU at the time that a new character is present to be loaded in the register.

overstriking Describes the capability of a printer to return to a specified character position on the paper in order to print the same or another character over an existing character.

overvoltage protection Circuitry to protect the computer's circuitry from undesirable increases in the AC power line voltage.

P Parity

PABX   Private Automatic Branch eXchange. A telephone switching system.

PACE   A 16-bit microprocessor (National Semiconductor).

package   A program or set of programs for a specific application which is prepared at one time to be used repeatedly at other times and/or by other people.

packed decimal   A means of data representation where two or more BCD digits are present in every word.

packet   A short block of data prefixed by length and destination information. It is the unit in which information is transferred in a packet-switching network.

packet-switching network   A network of devices which communicate by sending packets addressed to particular receivers.

pad   The rectangular contact area around the chip where the wire is bonded. *Also:* A character or characters inserted to fill a data field (usually a blank or blanks).

paging   In the case of a CRT, switching from one 'page' (i.e., a screen-full) of information to the next. In the case of a memory, a page is a logical block of storage used for memory management (for example, 1K words). In a paged system, a memory location is specified by a page address (number), and a displacement (address within the page). Rockwell uses paging with the PPS8 and National Semiconductor uses it in the NS16000.

PAL   Programmable Array Logic.

Mask programmed random logic circuitry.

parallel   The processing, transmission, or storage of data such that all of the elements of a compound item, such as the bits in a byte, are handled simultaneously.

parameter   A variable used to pass information to and from a subroutine or procedure. *Also:* A definable characteristic of a program or system.

parity   A one-bit quantity indicating whether the number of 1s in a word is even or odd. When parity is used, an actual extra bit is used with each word. This parity bit may be 1 when the parity is odd, 0 when it is even or vice-versa depending on the convention of the system designers. ASCII uses 7 bits for data and 1 bit for parity. Parity is one of the simplest error detection techniques, and will always detect a single-bit failure.

parser   A routine in charge of analysing a program statement and establishing its syntactic tree structure, according to the specified syntax of the programming language.

Pascal   A high-level programming language invented by Niklaus Wirth. Pascal is not an acronym; the language is named after the French mathematician and philosopher Blaise Pascal.

password   A unique sequence of alphanumeric characters assigned to the user of a computer system for identification and security purposes.

patch A section of code inserted into a program using unconditional transfers of control for purposes of debugging or alteration.

PBX Private Branch eXchange. telephone switching system.

PC Printed Circuit. *Also:* Program Counter.

PCB Printed Circuit Board. *Also:* PC-Board.

P-channel MOS (PMOS) The oldest LSI technology. It yields excellent component density, but is slower than NMOS.

PCM Pulse Code Modulation

PCS Personal Computing System

PDC Peripheral Device Controller, such as Rockwell's PIO.

PDP-11 One of the classical 16-bit minicomputers (made by DEC).

PE Parity Error. One of 5 status bits of a standard UART. It goes to 1 if received character parity does not match specified parity. *See:* FE, OR, DAV, TBMT.

PEEK A BASIC function which returns the contents of a particular memory location. *Also:* To look at the contents of memory.

peripheral Any device connected to a computer which is to some degree controlled by the computer.

personal computer A low-cost, portable computer with software oriented towards simple, single-user applications.

PET ["pet"] Personal Electronic Transaction computer. The Com-

modore Business Machines trademark for their home computer based on the 6502 microprocessor.

pf PicoFarad. Unit of capacitance.

PFR Power-Fail Restart

PGD Planar Gas Discharge display

phase The difference between the zero crossing or starting reference point of a standard waveform and that of the measured waveform. Phase is usually measured in degrees.

phase-locked oscillator (PLO) A phase-locked loop circuit used for precise data recovery in floppy disk drive controllers. The PLO stabilizes the separated data and clock bits.

photolithography The process currently used to print the masks on a wafer. It involves a photosensitive emulsion and selective etching techniques analogous to commercial lithography.

photoresist A chemical deposited on the silicon-dioxide layer of a wafer which, when exposed to a pattern of UV light, defines the areas to be etched.

PIA Motorola's name for a PIO.

PIC Priority Interrupt Controller. A special chip which manages several (usually 8) external interrupts, and provides automatic vectoring. It responds to the Interrupt-Acknowledge signal from the MPU by supplying one of n (usually n = 8) branching addresses, corresponding to the start address of an interrupt handler for the acknowledged interrupt.

pin-compatible Describes ICs which have identical functions and whose leads (or pins) are defined identically.

PIO Programmable Input-Output chip. A general 8-bit interface chip which multiplexes a single connection to the data bus into two or more 8-bit ports.

pipelining Describes computers which fetch the next instruction before completing execution of the previous instruction, in order to increase processor speed.

PIT Programmable Interval Timer. A chip equipped with a separate clock and several registers, used to count time independently of the MPU, for real-time applications. At the end of a time period, it sets a flag, generates an interrupt, or merely stores the time elapsed.

pixel An element of a picture, such as a dot on a video graphics display system.

PLA Programmable Logic Array. An LSI chip which can implement a combinatorial logic circuit involving (usually) over 10 inputs and eight outputs. The logic is determined by the internal masking of an AND matrix and an OR matrix. *See:* FPLA.

PL/I [*"pea-ell-one"*] Programming Language I, a language developed for IBM's 360 series in the mid-1960s. Digital Research produces a version for microprocessors.

PLL Phase Locked Loop

PL/M Programming Language for Microprocessors. A high-level language for microprocessors, originally developed by Intel. It is derived from XPL, a PL/I dialect.

PLO Phase Locked Oscillator

plotter A mechanical device for drawing images under computer control.

plug-compatible A term used to indicate when devices or components may be interchanged without requiring any modifications to the rest of the system.

PMI Precision Monolithics, Inc.

PMOS [*"pee-moss"*] P-channel Metal Oxide Semiconductor. *See:* P-channel MOS, NMOS, MOS.

p-n-p A transistor with an n-type substrate (in MOS implementation). The base and drain are p, i.e., doped with p-type impurities (excess electrons).

pointer An address used to point at a special entity or structure, e.g., program pointer or stack pointer. For 8-bit microprocessors, address pointers are generally 16 bits long so that they may specify up to 64K addresses. Pointers that point to fewer things may be shorter.

POKE A BASIC function which loads a particular memory location with a specified value. *Also:* To enter values into memory.

polling A scheduling technique for I/O devices in which the program interrogates the status of each polled device in turn, and gives service when required.

Other device service techniques are interrupt processing and DMA.

POP *["pop"]* An instruction used to remove a word from the top of the stack, usually to an accumulator.

port A physical I/O connection. For 8-bit microprocessors, it usually provides 8 bits of data at a time. *See:* channel.

POS Point-of-Sale. Refers to the ability to record commercial transactions at the point where they are made, e.g., at the cash register terminal.

positive logic True level is the voltage level most positive in the system. False level is the voltage level nearest zero. *See:* negative logic.

postfix A system of notation in which the operator follows the operand(s). *See:* RPN.

power down A sequence of steps taken by a computer when power fails or is shut off in order to preserve the state of the processor and prevent damage to peripherals.

power-fail restart A unit in charge of detecting a drop in the input voltage, and signaling an imminent power failure to the MPU. Several tens of milliseconds are still available during which all the registers can be preserved in non-volatile, or battery backed-up memory, allowing for an automatic orderly resumption of processing when power is restored.

power supply The unit that

converts the line voltage from the wall socket into the voltages required by the computer elements.

power up A sequence of steps taken by a computer when power is turned on or restored after a power failure. The CPU and peripherals are initialized and, if a power failure has occurred, the state of the processor is restored so that program execution may continue.

power-up diagnostics A set of programs, usually in ROM, which evaluate the condition of the CPU and memory on power-up.

PPI Intel's name for a PIO.

preprocessor A program or device which prepares data for further processing.

priority A number assigned to an event or device which determines the order in which it will receive service. By convention, 0 is the highest priority (usually assigned to power-fail detection). Also called a priority level.

probe An electrical device for making contact with a circuit test point for test or debugging purposes.

procedure A logically and functionally separate part of a program used to improve the readability, reliability, and structure of the program. Similar to a subroutine.

processor-bound Describes computation in which the internal processor speed is the limiting resource for programs. *Contrast with:* I/O-bound.

program A sequence of user-specified instructions which result in the execution of an algorithm. Programs are generally written at one of three levels: (1) binary or hexadecimal code (directly executable by the MPU), (2) assembly language (symbolic representation of the binary code, requiring an assembler), or (3) high-level language (requiring a compiler or interpreter, e.g., BASIC.).

program counter A register which contains the address of the next instruction to be executed. A program counter is incremented after each instruction is fetched for execution and can be modified by transfer instructions within a program, such as subroutine calls. *See:* register, CPU.

programming language A language used to write a program, which may be assembly level or high level.

PROM [*"prom"*] Programmable Read-Only Memory. A ROM that may be altered by the user. *See:* PROM programmer, read-only memory.

PROM programmer A module or external device used to write bit patterns in a user-programmable PROM. Input may be through a hex keyboard, binary paper tape, or directly from an MDS.

propagate Pass through a system from one component to another. *Also:* One of the two signals supplied by an adder, for carry prediction by a carry look-ahead circuit.

propagation delay The time required for a pulse or a level transition to propagate through a device.

proportional spacing A method of printing in which the amount of horizontal space allocated to each character is dependent on the width of the character. Proportionally spaced type appears typeset and is more legible than fixed-width type.

protected field Describes a means of specifying areas of a CRT screen which cannot be modified by direct keyboard entries from the operator.

protocol A set of rules governing the exchange of information between two systems.

pseudo-instruction A user-defined instruction, such as a listing control or a macro, which does not belong to the basic instruction set of the MPU. It is directed to and interpreted by the assembler. Also called a 'directive'.

PSW Program Status Word. It contains the carry flag, zero flag, and other relevant information on the state of the central processor.

PTP Paper Tape Punch. A once popular output device producing machine-readable output data in the form of holes punched in a paper tape. *See:* PTR.

PTR Paper Tape Reader. A formerly popular low cost input device. The PTP/PTR combination has been largely replaced by cassette tape units.

pull-up resistor Provides the source current for open-collector logic gates or terminating unused high inputs.

pulse Voltage or current which lasts for a short period of time and is square or Gaussian in shape.

pulser A circuit delivering high-current short duration signals to a unit under test.

PUSH [*"push"*] The instruction used to deposit a word on top of a stack.

pushdown list Stack

PWB Printed Wire Board

PWM Pulse Width Modulation

Q Half-width of power spectrum of bandpass filter response in hertz, divided into the center frequency in hertz. *Also:* A register used as an accumulator extension, necessary for efficient multiply-divide operations and not generally provided in earlier 8-bit MPUs. Newer 8-bit and 16-bit MPUs generally have a larger set of general purpose registers than the older 8-bit MPUs having an A register/Q register combination.

QA Quality Assurance

Q Bus The internal system bus of the DEC LSI-11 computer.

QC Quality Control

QPL Qualified Products List. 38510—Military qualified products list for high reliability applications.

QTAM [*"queue-tam"*] Queued

Teleprocessing Access Method (IBM term).

quad Involving four entities.

quad density Specifies storage density of a disk medium. Quad density stores four times the amount of information per disk as single density.

queue A FIFO data structure to which items are added at one end, and removed from the other. Queues are often used to organize tasks waiting to be processed.

QUIP [*"qwip"*] QUad In-line Package. An IC package with two rows of pins on each side which is much smaller than a comparable DIP.

QUME A manufacturer of computer peripherals.

QWERTY [*"qwer-tee"*] The traditional typewriter keyboard layout, in which the keys for those six letters appear in one of the rows in that order.

R Reset. *Also:* Register. *Also:* Request. *Also:* Ring indicator.

rack mountable Describes equipment packaged for installation in a metal cabinet called a rack.

radiation hardening A quality assurance process used in the production of ICs to select those circuits which are better able to withstand radiation.

Radio Shack A manufacturer of electronic parts and equipment, including the TRS-80 line of computers.

RALU [*"ral-loo"*] Register-equipped ALU. A bit-slice ancestor (National Semiconductor).

RAM Random Access Memory. It denotes, in fact, Read/Write memory.

random access An access method where each word can be retrieved directly by its address, independent of any other word.

RAS [*"raz"*] Row Address Strobe. A signal used in dynamic RAMs to reduce the pin count by multiplexing the address.

raster scan (CRT display) A standard TV display technique where an image is built from aggregates of dots of varying intensities.

RATFOR [*"rat-for"*] RATional FORtran. A structured dialect of FORTRAN which is compiled into standard FORTRAN by a preprocessor.

R-C Resistor-Capacitor. A circuit connected to an oscillator to define its oscillating frequency. For stable frequencies, a crystal is necessary.

RD Received Data (RS-232C standard).

RDE Received Data Enable. A status flag on a UART.

RDOS [*"are-doss"*] Real-time Disc-Operating System. *See:* DOS.

RDY A control signal used with slow memory to indicate valid data.

read-only memory (ROM) Storage which can be written only once. The information is then fixed and cannot be changed. A ROM is mask-programmed by the manufacturer.

read/write Describes the nature of an operation, i.e., the direction of data flow.

real-time An action or system capable of action at a speed commensurate with the time of occurrence of an actual process.

real-time operating system An operating system capable of real-time task management, including event scheduling, interrupt management, and real-time event counters.

reasonableness test A test that the value of a variable falls within a bracket defined as reasonable. It is used to detect and filter noisy inputs or erroneous outputs.

record A unit of information, either read, written or stored, such as a punched card, a disk sector, or a line of characters.

recursive Refers to a function, routine, or procedure which calls itself.

redundancy The use of more than one of the same item to increase reliabilty or performance.

reentrant Pertaining to programs or routines written in reentrant code. *See:* reentrant code.

reentrant code A single segment of code and data which is not modified during execution, so that it may be called by multiple programs.

refresh The logic necessary to rewrite the contents of the complete dynamic RAM periodically, typically every 2 ms.

refresh circuitry Electronic circuitry which periodically reads and rewrites the contents of dynamic memory to prevent loss of data. *See:* dynamic memory.

register One word of memory, usually implemented in fast flip-flops, directly accessible to a processor. Most MPUs include a set of internal registers which can be accessed much faster than the main memory.

register select One or more lines used to select one register out of a given number within a device. Register select pins are normally connected to the address bus.

relative addressing A method of memory addressing in which the information desired is located by adding a displacement from a pointer to the pointer itself. In other words, addresses are expressed relative to some base address or pointer.

relocatable The load module or object form of a program or routine which does not contain fixed addresses, or which is structured so that it can be 'relocated' and executed anywhere in the memory.

rem A unit of radiation.

RES RESet signal

reset To return to zero, or to some arbitrarily selected beginning point.

resident (software) A program which resides in the main memory of the system. It is convenient to have the editor, the assembler, and the debugger resident in main memory simultaneously.

retrofit To improve or change software or hardware by making additions.

RETURN An instruction used to terminate a subroutine. It returns control to, i.e., causes execution to resume at, the next instruction following the subroutine call.

reverse video The ability of some CRT terminals to display dark characters on a light background as opposed to the standard light on dark.

RFI Radio-Frequency Interference

RF modulator A device which encodes a composite video signal, as output by many hobbyist microcomputers, into a radio frequency signal for display on a standard television set.

RFP Request For Proposals

RFQ Request For Quotes

RI Right In. The right input to a shifter.

ripple-carry An addition technique where the carry coming out of an adder is propagated to the next adder. A faster method is to use carry look-ahead.

rise time The time required to complete the low-to-high transition of a pulse.

RMS Root Mean Square, an averaging technique.

RMW Read-Modify-Write cycle in a RAM memory.

RO Right Out. The right output from a shifter.

rollover Depressing two or more keys on a keyboard simultaneously. A good keyboard controller must include debouncing and multiple-key rollover protection.

ROM [*"romm"*] Read-Only Memory

ROMable Describes code which will execute properly when placed in ROM memory: segments of ROMable code do not modify themselves, and do not include temporary data storage areas.

ROTATE An instruction which shifts the contents of a register or word to the left or right. The bit coming in one end of the rotating word is generally the one falling off the other end. Sometimes, it is the old value of the carry bit (9-bit rotation).

round-robin A scheduling technique in which a task list is cycled through from top to bottom and back again. In round-robin scheduling each process or device corresponding to a task is guaranteed periodic service whatever the actual task traffic may be.

routine A section of code written to perform a specific action, such as an input character routine, or a square root routine.

row scanning A technique used in decoding which key of a keyboard was pressed. Each row is scanned in turn by outputting a 1. The output on the columns is examined, resulting in identification of the key.

RPG Report Program Generator. A business-oriented programming language.

RPM Rotations Per Minute

RPN Reverse Polish Notation. *See:* postfix notation.

RPROM [*"are-promm"*] (User) Reprogrammable Read Only Memory. *See:* PROM.

RS Register Select

R-S flip flop A flip-flop using two cross-coupled NAND gates.

RS-232C The widely used standard for connecting computer system components, especially for serial communication of control and data between computers and serial input/output peripheral devices. Actually RS-232C is an electrical standard for connecting data terminal equipment (DTEs) such as CRTs (or computers) to data communication equipment (DCEs) such as modems or network data concentrators. *See:* EIA RS-232C.

RTC Real Time Clock. A time counter used to measure the duration of an event. It is independent from the processor and not affected by interrupts.

RTOS Real Time Operating System

RTS Ready To Send (RS-232C standard signal).

run Refers to the execution of a program on a computer.

R/W Read/Write

RZ Return to Zero. A recording technique.

S Select. *Also:* Strobe.

S-100 An extremely widespread 100-line microcomputer system bus. It was originally developed as the bus for the first 8080-based hobbyist system, Altair. It has since been standardized as the IEEE 696 bus. In its latest form, it may be used with the newer 16-bit microprocessors.

sample and hold An analog circuit to capture and retain a signal so that it may be converted by an A/D.

sampling Measuring an input value at intervals.

satellite processor A computer subordinate to another computer, possibly communicating over large distances, which performs specialized processing related to the master computer.

SBC Single Board Computer. A name generally applied to a line of board-level products built to Intel specifications and using a common system bus known as the multibus. This bus is being standardized as the IEEE 796. National Semiconductor has a compatible board line designated by the letters BLC (Board-Level-Computer).

SCCS Southern California Computer Society

scheduling Allocating the time of a module.

Schottky A technology of high-speed circuits.

SC/MP [*"scamp"*] Simple Cost-effective MicroProcessor. National Semiconductor's small 8-bit microprocessor.

scope The scope of a variable or definition is that part of the program in which it may be ac-

cessed. *Also:* an abbreviation for oscilloscope.

Scotch A brand of magnetic recording media.

SCR Silicon Controlled Rectifier

scratchpad A group of general purpose registers without specific function that serve as a high speed workspace for some operations; usually, it is an internal RAM.

screen generator A program which aids in the definition of CRT screen forms, which are a particular pattern of symbols on a CRT screen for purposes of data entry and display. Screen forms are often displayed in protected fields.

screen size A measure of the amount of information that a CRT screen can display. Screens may be measured diagonally, as TV sets, or by the number of vertical and horizontal dot or character positions.

scrolling Moving the contents of the CRT screen up or down by one or more lines.

SDLC Synchronous Data Link Control. An IBM computer networking protocol.

SE Sign Extend. A technique used during a multiply or divide operation and during some shift operations to insure that negative numbers remain negative when shifted right. The convention is that bits shifted into the high end of the register will be identical to the bit that was in the high order position when the shift began.

second source   The manufacturer of a device, other than the original one.

sector   A contiguous section of a disk track. A block of data on a disk is addressed by its track and sector numbers. Typical disk sector sizes are 128, 256 or 512 bytes of data. Consecutively numbered sectors may or may not be physically adjacent within a track.

seek time   The time needed to position the head of a disk over the specified track.

segment   A contiguous block of memory addresses, such as 0 to 64K.

sensor   A device which translates a physical stimulus into an electronic signal which may, for example, be input into a computer.

sequencer   In a bit-slice system, the module in charge of providing the next microprogram address to the microprogram memory. It is essentially a complex multiplexer, but may include stack facilities and a loop counter.

sequential access   An access method in which items (words or records) may be accessed in a fixed order only. The standard example of a sequentially accessed medium is magnetic tape where, in order to access a particular record, all records before it must be scanned first.

sequential file   A file whose elements may only be accessed in ascending order. In order to read an element of a sequential file, all of the preceding elements must be accessed.

serial   The processing, transmission, or storage of data such that all of the elements of a compound item, such as the bits in a byte, are handled sequentially. *Contrast with:* parallel.

serial data   Data transmitted sequentially, one bit at a time.

serial port   An I/O port through which data is transmitted and received serially. Serial ports are often used for communicating with terminals.

series   Circuit elements connected so that the output of one is the input of the next.

setup time   The time required before a signal can be changed from its prior state.

S/H   Sample and Hold

shell   The name for the command interpreter running under the Unix operating system.

shift   Moving the contents of a register left or right by one bit or more. The bit falling out goes into the carry ("C") bit of the status register or is lost. The bit coming in is usually a 0, except in some special circumstances such as Sign-Extend.

shift register   A register whose contents can be moved left or right by one or more bit positions.

SI   Serial Input

side effect   An unintentional change to the value of a global variable by a function, procedure, or subroutine. Structured programming languages discourage side effects by limiting the scope of global variables.

sign Plus or minus. In two's-complement notation, the sign can be determined by examining bit 7, the MSB.

signed binary A binary representation of signed integer numbers which sets aside one bit, usually the high-order or leftmost bit, to indicate the sign of the number.

sign magnitude A binary representation for integers where the MSB acts as the sign (0 for "+", 1 for "−") and the rest of the bits contain the magnitude, or absolute value, of the number.

silicon-gate The MOS technology using silicon for the gate of the transistor. An alternative is aluminum-gate.

Silicon Valley The area around Sunnyvale, in the Santa Clara Valley of California, where many semiconductor manufacturers are located. More generally, it contains the greatest concentration of electronics industries in the U.S. It is also called Silicon Gulch, but never Silicone Valley.

simplex Data transferred in one direction only.

simulator A program with the same input/output behavior as the device it simulates, but generally slower. A simulated time counter allows the measurement of time. An MPU is easily simulated but I/O cannot be precisely simulated because of timing considerations, so only

the logic of a program can be tested with a simulator.

single board computer A complete computer on one printed circuit board: CPU, ROM, RAM, and interfaces. Single board computers are often used for industrial control applications.

single precision arithmetic Regular arithmetic, e.g., arithmetic on single-word integers, by contrast to double or multi-precision arithmetic.

single sided A method of disk storage using only one side of the disk. *Also:* A printed-circuit board with printed-circuit wiring on only one side.

single-stepping Refers to the execution of a program one statement or step at a time. It is useful for debugging.

sink current A logic family's current drive capability. Sink current is 1.6 milliamperes for one standard TTL gate.

SIP Single In-line Package

skip An instruction to skip the following program instruction. A condition is usually specified, such as: "SKIP IF Z TRUE".

slave Any device under the control of another device, or imitating its operation.

slew rate A fast signal response measured in volts per second, and used in operational amplifier specifications.

slice See: bit-slice.

SLSI Super Large Scale Integration. A technology which holds

100,000 transistors per chip.

small scale integration (SSI)
The technology which holds one to ten gates per device.

Smalltalk A language and software system developed by the Learning Research Group at the Xerox Palo Alto Research Center (PARC) during the years 1971-1980. It was released in 1981. Smalltalk is organized around two fundamental concepts: objects and messages. Smalltalk systems are characterized by a high degree of graphical interaction.

SMI Static Memory Interface

smoke test Turning on the equipment for the first time to see if it will operate.

SMS Scientific Micro Systems, a manufacturer.

SNOBOL [*"snow-ball"*] StriNg-Oriented symBOlic Language. A character-string manipulation programming language.

SNR Signal to Noise Ratio

SO Serial Output

SO Shift-Out bit

SOB Start-Of-Block

socket A mechanical electrical connector. The socket is also known as the female connector.

soft-fail The techniques which preserve a degree of system operation despite failures.

soft-sectored A disk format where the beginning of every sector is detected by reading magnetic marks on the disk. This is in contrast to hard-sectored where each sector's origin is marked by a physical hole.

software The instructions that tell hardware what to do with data, i.e., the programs. *Contrast with:* hardware.

software-compatible
Describes MPUs which execute the same instructions (i.e., have the same machine language).

software package A pre-written group of commercially available programs designed to serve a specific need, such as word processing, inventory control, data base management, etc.

SOH Start Of Header

solder mask A printed circuit board technique where everything is coated with plastic except the contacts to be soldered.

solid state Characterizes electronic devices which function by diffusion of electrons through solid materials. Includes transistors, diodes, and registers, but not vacuum tubes.

Soroc A brand of CRT terminals.

sort To arrange items according to defined criteria, such as alphabetical or numerical order.

SOS Silicon-On-Sapphire. Integrated circuit technology in which a sapphire substrate is used yielding high speeds of operation.

source The emitter of a transistor.

source code A program as it is submitted to an assembler or compiler. It is almost always a file containing ASCII or other characters.

source language The original language used by the programmer, on which a translator program operates to produce a version (object code) in the language used by the machine.

SP Stack Pointer

space Binary 0. In the RS-232C standard, negative voltage; in a current loop, no current flow; and in modems, the lower frequency of the pair. See: mark. Also: Commonly used as a synonym for the blank character.

SPDT Single Pole Double Throw. A type of switch.

spikes Sharp, temporary increases in a signal or voltage.

Spinwriter A line of thimble printers manufactured by Nippon Electric Corporation.

split screen Division of a CRT screen into two or more separate areas, or windows, in which distinct information is displayed.

spool Simultaneous Peripheral Operations On-Line. A method of increasing system throughput by allowing programs using slow output devices to complete execution rapidly. Program output data is placed in queues on high-speed mass storage devices for low-speed transmission concurrent with normal system operation.

SPST Single Pole Single Throw. A type of switch.

SR Status Register

SS Solid State

SSDA Synchronous Serial Data Adaptor. A synchronous serial interface.

SSI Small Scale Integration. A technology holding a few gates per element.

SSR Solid State Relay

stack A LIFO structure which preserves the chronological ordering of information and is necessary for subroutines and interrupt management. A stack is manipulated by two basic instructions, PUSH and POP.

stack pointer The register in the CPU which contains the address of the top of the stack in memory.

stand-alone A device which will operate by itself, requiring no other equipment.

start bit A bit indicating the beginning of asynchronous serial transmission. See: stop bit.

statement A string of characters which is syntactically complete with respect to a high-level language translator.

state table A list of the outputs of a logic circuit based on the inputs and the previous outputs. Such a circuit has memory and cannot be described by a simple truth table. Also called state-transition table.

static memory MOS memory which uses a flip-flop as a storage element. It does not need to be refreshed and does not require a clock. It does not lose its contents as long as power is applied.

static RAM Memory circuits

which retain their contents as long as power is applied.

status The present condition of the device, usually indicated by flag flip-flops in special registers. *See:* flag.

status bit handshaking The delegation of certain bits of a parallel I/O port to coordinate information transfer with a peripheral device. Status bits are used to signify device read, buffer full, printer out of paper, etc.

status register A register used to hold status information inside a functional unit, such as an MPU, a PIC, a DMAC, or an FDC. A typical MPU status register provides: carry, overflow, sign (negative), zero, and interrupt. It can also include parity, enable (interrupts), and mask.

STD STanDard

stepper motor A mechanical device which rotates by a fixed amount each time it is pulsed.

stop bit A bit indicating the end of asynchronous serial transmission.

strain gauge A sensor which produces a voltage or resistance change when a force is applied.

string An ordered sequence of data items, such as characters. For example, the word 'string' is a string of six characters. *See:* character string.

string handling The capability of a programming language to operate on strings of characters.

strobe A selection signal that is active when data are correct on a bus.

structured language A computer language designed to aid or enforce structured programming. Control structures such as IF...THEN...ELSE, DO...WHILE, and REPEAT...UNTIL, together with provisions for declaring logically separate program modules such as procedures, and limiting the scope of variables all lend a modular structure to programs. Unconditional control transfer statements are often left unimplemented. Popular structured languages are PASCAL, ALGOL, and C.

structured programming A set of techniques designed to increase the reliability and comprehensibility of programs by increasing programmer discipline. Structured programming involves precise problem specification, top-down or stepwise program design, and block-structured or modular programs.

STTL Standard Transistor-Transistor Logic. Example: 7400 series logic is STTL.

STX Start of TeXt

sub-harmonic A fractional multiple of the fundamental frequency.

subroutine A program segment identified by name and bracketed by a 'subroutine' and a 'return' statement. Execution is transferred to a subroutine when a subroutine call occurs. Subroutines improve program modularity and save memory space at a minimal cost in the overhead required to process the call/return sequence.

support chips   All the components beyond the main device required for complete system operation.

SUT   Socket Under Test

SW   Status Word

switching regulator   A power supply design in which efficient regulation is performed by commuting the input voltage into a filter circuit.

SYBEX   A leading publisher of computer books.

symbolic   Describes the use of characters or character strings in a defined syntax to stand for machine-related constructs such as instructions or data.

symbol table   A table constructed by an assembler or compiler to associate symbolic names to actual addresses or values.

sync   Short for synchronous or synchronizing.

synchronous   Operation controlled by a mutually sensed clock pulse. *See:* clock.

synchronous system   A system in which all events are synchronized by a common clock pulse.

syntax   The set of grammatical rules defining valid constructs of a language.

system   Any aggregate of two or more interconnected electronic components. Also used informally for 'computer system'. *See:* computer system.

system-controller   An Intel 8228 chip required to demultiplex the 8080's data bus into separate streams of data (8 lines) and control information (5 lines).

T   An electrical network shaped like the letter "T" with one input, one output and one ground lead. It is used with resistors for attenuators and capacitors, and inductors for filters. *Also:* True—a logical 1.

tabbing   A method of moving a CRT cursor or printer head to a prespecified column on the screen or paper, called a tab stop.

table look-up   The process of finding a value in a table. This process is most efficient when indexed addressing facilities are available.

tape (magnetic)   An inexpensive mass storage medium with the disadvantage of requiring sequential access. It is convenient for large files, or archival storage.

task   A particular execution of a program.

TBMT   Transmitter Buffer eMpTy. One of the 5 status bits of a standard UART. It becomes true when a buffer may be reloaded. *See:* PE, FE, OR, DAV.

TCAM   [*"tee-cam"*]   TeleCommunications Access Method (IBM term).

TCP   Transmitter Clock

TD   Transmitted Data (RS-232C standard).

TDM   Time-Division Multiplexing

TDMA   Time Division Multiple Access

teletype   One of the oldest, most cost-effective and most reliable peripherals for communication with a computer, but with the disadvantage of being slow (10 characters per second or 110 baud).

TEMP   TEMPorary

terminal mode   A mode of operation of a general purpose computer such that its CRT and/or printer can be used as a terminal for another computer.

text editor   See: editor.

thermistor   A temperature sensor which changes resistance with temperature.

thick film   A method of hybrid fabrication in which the chips are mounted and interconnected on a ceramic substrate.

thimble printer   A printer using a printing element similar to a daisy-wheel. The spokes, however, are bent up out of the plane of rotation forming a cup- or thimble-shaped element with the die-cast type facing outward.

thin film   A method of hybrid fabrication in which devices are placed on top of the chip itself.

threaded   Describes programs made up of calls to many separate subroutines.

three-address instruction   An instruction which can specify separately two sources and a destination.

throughput   The number of instructions executed per second or some other measure of execution efficiency.

TI   Texas Instruments, the largest manufacturer of semiconductors. TI is also active in the areas of computer systems and consumer electronics.

time-division multiple access   A signal transmission technique used to increase the traffic capacity of satellites.

time-division multiplexing   A multiplexing technique where each time slot is allocated to a separate device or function. It may be used in conjunction with other techniques to increase the throughput.

time sharing system   See: TSS.

tiny BASIC   A reduced subset of the BASIC programming language which provides only integer arithmetic and limited string operations. It fits in 4K bytes of memory.

TOD   Time Of Day. See: real-time clock.

touch sensitive   Characterizes switches which can be activated by touching a conductive surface. Many computer input devices use touch-sensitive switches.

tpi   Tracks Per Inch. A unit used to measure track density in floppy disks.

trace   A 'wire' on a printed-circuit board. Also: Monitoring and displaying or storing the state of a system step-by-step as a process is carried out.

track   One of the rings defined on the magnetic surface of a disk or drum. A floppy disk may have 77 tracks, numbered from 0 to 76.

tractor feed   A method of accurately positioning and transporting fan-fold paper in printers. The edges of the paper have perforations which engage with sprocket wheels in the printer's paper transport mechanism.

transaction   A short dialog between a computer and an operator for a specific purpose, such as making an airline reservation, noting an inventory change, or interrogating a data base.

transient   An intermediate unstable state.

translator   A generic term for compiler or assembler.

trap   A method of catching program errors when illegal instructions are executed or illegal memory locations are accessed. *Also:* A mode in which the computer interrupts itself after each instruction to allow a trace or other diagnostic program to operate.

triac   A thyristor for AC power control.

trim-pot   A variable resistor with screwdriver adjustment.

tristate   (Trademark of National Semiconductor)   Three-state logic; that is, logic which can be in one of three logical states: "0" (low), "1" (high), and undefined or floating (high-impedance). Most microprocessor data and address buses are tristate.

TRS-80   A line of computers made by Tandy Corp. (Radio Shack) using the Z80 microprocessor.

TRSDOS   [*"triss-doss"*] The standard disk operating system for TRS-80 computers.

truth table   A table listing the output values as a function of all possible combinations of input values.

TSB   A signal which sets the number of stop bits on a standard UART to 1 or 2.

TSO   Time-Sharing Option (IBM term).

TSS   Time-Sharing System. A computer operating system in which the processor's time is shared among simultaneous users, allowing an interactive programming environment.

TTL   Transistor-Transistor Logic

TTY   TeleTYpe or TeleTYpewriter

Turing, Alan M.   A British scientist who demonstrated in the 1930's that all functions could be built out of 3 gates: AND, OR, and NOT.

turtlegraphics   A method of creating graphic images on a display or output device by sending commands to a "turtle", represented by a cursor on a CRT screen or plotter pen, etc. The turtle can be instructed to simulate the action of drawing with a pen as it moves.

TUT   Transistor Under Test

TV   TeleVision

TVT   TeleVision Typewriter terminal

two-port RAMs A RAM memory system with two access channels. Two-port memory is often used for memory-mapped video display systems, where both the processor and the video display circuitry must have access to the memory holding the screen image.

two's-complement A method of expressing binary numbers in which the negative of a number is generated by complementing the number and adding 1. Standard binary arithmetic (+ or −) can be used without special provision for the sign indicated by the MSB.

TWT Traveling Wave Tube. It is used for generating microwave radio frequencies.

U Underflow. *Also:* A lowercase u is sometimes used to represent the Greek letter mu (μ) in the context meaning micro.

UART [*"you-art"*] Universal Asynchronous Receiver/Transmitter. A serial-to-parallel, and parallel-to-serial, converter. Usually, a particular kind of IC, used to interface a byte-parallel port to a bit-serial communications network.

UHF Ultra High Frequencies

Unibus A classic minicomputer bus, with more than 100 signals invented by DEC for its PDP-11. It is not used by the LSI-11. (Trademark of Digital Equipment Corporation.)

Unix A mini- and microcomputer operating system developed by Bell Labs which features multiprogramming, a hierarchical file structure, and numerous useful utilities. *See:* Xenix.

unstack Same as POP. To remove from the top of a stack.

uP Microprocessor

UPC Universal Product Code

UPI Universal Peripheral Interface

upward compatible Describes equipment or software which, when improved, will have features that are a superset of their original features.

us Microsecond = 10^{-6}s

USART [*"you-sart"*] Universal Synchronous/Asynchronous Receiver/Transmitter. A chip which handles all the operations associated with synchronous data communications, such as bisync.

USASCII Same as ASCII. *See:* ASCII.

USASCII-8 Same as ASCII. *See:* ASCII.

USRT Universal Synchronous Receiver/Transmitter. A serial to parallel converter for high-speed communications.

utilities The software used for routine tasks. Utilities are designed to facilitate or aid the operation and use of the computer. Examples of utilities are an editor, a debugger, and a file handler.

UUT Unit Under Test

UV UltraViolet

V Volt. *Also:* The overflow status flag.

variable A symbolically named entity which may assume an assigned value, or a number of values.

VAX A 32-bit minicomputer manufactured by digital Equipment, which is also capable of executing PDP-11 machine language.

VDI Video Display Input

VDT Video Display Terminal. The term used in the newspaper community for CRT.

VDU Video Display Unit. The British term for CRT.

vectored interrupt An interrupt which carries its identity number, or the address of its handler.

vectoring Automatic branching to a specified address. *See:* interrupt.

V/F Voltage to Frequency converter

VHF Very High Frequencies

VIC 20 A low-end personal color-output computer from Commodore Business Machines.

video signal An electronic signal containing information on the location and brightness of each position on a CRT screen, along with timing signals to place the image properly on the screen.

VIP An RCA board using the COSMAC MPU.

virtual address A user-generated address which references objects in a logical (virtual) address space regardless of the physical memory location where they reside. A virtual address must be

translated by the operating system into a valid physical address which may, in turn, involve the movement of data between primary and secondary storage.

virtual memory The memory address space available to any process in execution on the processor. It may be larger than the physical memory.

VisiCalc A software package marketed by Personal Software, which is designed to aid solution of mathematical problems by allowing the user to set up an "electronic sheet," or grid of rows and columns on the video screen. Locations within the grid can be treated as variables and equations for solving complex problems can be applied to these variables.

VLSI Very Large Scale Integration. A technology holding over 10,000 transistors per chip.

VMOS [*"vee-moss"*] Vertical MOS. The technology used to increase the density of components per square mil, where a V-shaped groove is cut in the silicon substrate.

volatile storage Storage which loses its contents when power is removed.

VOM Volt Ohm Milliammeter. A test instrument for measuring voltage, resistance, and current. It is usually portable, with an analog meter for readout.

VSS Voltage for Substrate and Sources, the ground for MOS circuits.

VSYNC [*"vee-sink"*] Vertical

SYNC signal in a TV. It determines the vertical position of the image displayed.

VTAM [*"vee-tam"*] Virtual Teleprocessing Access Method (IBM 370).

VTR   Video Tape Recorder

W   Write

wafer   A slice of a silicon ingot on which integrated circuits are fabricated. After testing and fabrication, the wafer is cut up into individual circuit dice or chips. The dice that were not rejected in the wafer test are then packaged and further sorted and tested before being offered as finished IC components. *See:* chip, silicon.

wait state   A micro-cycle or internal state entered by an MPU when a synchronizing signal is not present. It is used to synchronize a faster processor with a slow memory.

wand   A stick used to read the optically coded product labels (bar-code) found on retail sales items.

WD   Western Digital Corporation, a manufacturer of processor and controller chips.

WE   Write Enable

WEMA   [*"wee-ma"*] Western Electronics Manufacturers Association

Winchester disk   A hard disk system characterized by very light read/write heads, low head-to-disk clearance, and complete enclosure of the magnetic media in a dust-free environment to achieve high information density and fast access-time.

window   A section of a CRT screen dedicated to displaying specific types of information. *See:* split screen.

wire wrap   A mechanical method for connecting wires in complex circuits. Each wire is tightly wound several turns around square posts to make the electrical connection. This technology is now used mostly for hardware during system development.

WOM   [*"womm"*] Write Only Memory

word   A logical unit of information. It may have any number of bits, but for MPUs, a word is usually 4, 8, 16, or 32 bits.

word processor   A computer-based system for writing, editing, and formatting letters, reports, and books.

WordStar   A complete word processing package from MicroPro. This book was developed using WordStar.

workspace   An area of memory allocated for working storage, i.e., an area without predetermined use.

wpm   Words Per Minute

write-protect   Describes the act of preventing information from being written onto a storage medium. Floppy disk jackets often have adhesive tabs which can be removed (for 8" disks) or placed on the disk (for 5-1/4" disks) to write-protect the disk by disabling the disk drive's write circuitry.

WS   Workspace

WV   Working Voltage

X   Index Register

XENIX   [*"zee-nicks"*] The Microsoft implementation of the Unix operating system for microcomputers.

XMT   TransMiT

XMIT   TransMIT

XR   EXternal Reset

XTAL   CrysTAL

x-y plotter   A device which draws points or lines on a sheet of paper when given x and y coordinates by a computer.

yield   The proportion of operational chips in a batch, i.e., the ratio of good chips to total chips on a wafer.

Z   Impedance measured in ohms. *Also:* The Zero flag.

THE NUMBERS GAME

371   Cassette controller. (NEC)

372   FDC (NEC)

400   4-bit I^2L slice. (TI)

401   4-bit slice. (TI)

601   16-bit chip. (Data General)

1000   4-bit microprocessor available in the various versions listed below. Also called TMS-1000. (TI)

1070   *See:* 1000.

1100   *See:* 1000.

1200   *See:* 1000.

1270   *See:* 1000.

1300   *See:* 1000.

1600   Chip set designed for PDP-11/03 emulation. (Western Digital)

1702   An ultraviolet-erasable PROM organized as 256 words by 8 bits.

1771   Single density floppy disk controller chip.

1791   Double density floppy disk controller chip.

1802   Cosmac 8-bit CMOS microprocessor. (RCA)

2102   Common static RAM integrated circuit, organized as 1K $\times$ 1 bit.

2114   Static RAM organized as 1K $\times$ 4 bits.

2650   8-bit microprocessor. (Signetics)

2651   2650 UART. (Signetics)

2652   SDLC chip. (Signetics)

2655   2650 PIO. (Signetics)

2702   See: 1702.

2708   An ultraviolet-erasable PROM organized as 1K $\times$ 8 bits.

2716   An ultraviolet-erasable PROM organized as 2K $\times$ 16 bits. (Intel)

2716   An ultraviolet-erasable PROM organized as 2K $\times$ 8 bits.

Not compatible with the Intel part. (TI)

2732   An ultraviolet-erasable PROM organized as 4K × 8 bits.

2900 A family of 4-bit slice components. Widely used to construct special-purpose controllers and microprocessors. Introduced by AMD and second-sourced by many other manufacturers.

2901   A 4-bit slice processor. (AMD)

2902   Look-ahead carry generator. (AMD)

2903   An improved version of 2901. (AMD)

2909   Microprogram sequencer. (AMD)

2911   Microprogram sequencer. (AMD)

2914   PIC (AMD)

3000   Family of 2-bit slice components. (Intel)

3001   Microprogram control unit. (Intel)

3002   Central processing element 2-bit slice. (Intel)

3003   Look-ahead carry generator. (Intel)

3850   The F8 family processor chip. Part of an 8-bit two-chip microcomputer. (Fairchild)

3851   The F8 family program storage unit used with the 3850. (Fairchild)

3852   Dynamic memory interface for the F8. (Fairchild)

3853   SMI for the F8. (Fairchild)

3854   DMA for the F8. (Fairchild)

3861   PIO for the F8. (Fairchild)

3870   An 8-bit one-chip microcomputer. Upgrade of the 3870, contains 4032 bytes of ROM, and 128 bytes of RAM. (Mostek)

3876   An 8-bit one-chip microcomputer. Upgrade of the 3870, contains 4032 bytes of ROM, and 256 bytes of RAM. (Mostek)

3880   Mostek Z80.

4004   4-bit microprocessor. (Intel)

4040   4-bit microprocessor. Upgrade of the 4004, contains more registers and executes a larger instruction set. (Intel)

4044   Static RAM organized as 4K × 1 bit.

4116   Dynamic RAM organized as 16K × 1 bit.

4164   Dynamic RAM organized as 64K × 1 bit.

4264   4040 PIO.

4308   ROM (1K × 8) + I/O ports for the 4040. (Intel)

5701   MMI 4-bit slice predecessor of the 2901 (mil version).

6100   Intersil 12-bit CMOS microprocessor which emulates the PDP-8.

6502   8-bit microprocessor. Widely used in mass-marketed computer systems, such as Apple, Pet, and Atari. (MOS Technology)

65XX   Support chips belonging to the 6502 family. (MOS)

6520   PIO (MOS Technology)

6530   RAM, ROM, I/O and timer. (MOS Technology)

6701 Same as the 5701 in the commercial version.

6800 8-bit microprocessor. (Motorola)

6801 8-bit one-chip microcomputer.

6802 8-bit two-chip microcomputer. Upgrade of the 6800, contains functions that were previously in the other 6800 family components. (Motorola)

6809 8-bit high performance upgrade of the 6800. Has an expanded instruction set and 16-bit word handling capability. (Motorola)

6820 6800 PIO. (Motorola, Fairchild, Mostek)

6828 PIC (Motorola)

6845 CRT controller. (Motorola)

6850 6800 UART. (Motorola)

6860 Modem. (Motorola, Fairchild, AMD)

6870 Clock. (Motorola)

7400 Series of TTL logic. (TI)

8008 8-bit microprocessor. (Intel)

8048 8-bit family of one-chip microcomputers with one-chip RAM and ROM. The 8748 version has an EPROM on the same chip as the processor. (Intel)

8080 8-bit microprocessor. Upgrade from the 8008, has a different instruction set but retains a similar architecture to the 8008. The 8080 was the dominant microprocessor of the 1970s. (Intel)

8085 8-bit microprocessor. Upgrade of the 8080, contains functions that were previously on other 8080 family chips as well as two extra instructions and four interrupt levels. (Intel)

8086 16-bit byte-oriented microprocessor that resembles the 8085, but has an expanded instruction set and 16-bit arithmetic capabilities. (Intel)

8087 Numeric data co-processor for the 8086 and the 8088. Implements proposed IEEE floating-point standard.

8088 8086 microprocessor with 8-bit external data paths. (Intel)

8089 16-bit input/output processor. (Intel)

8212 Parallel latch and buffer in the 8080 family. (Intel)

8224 Clock generator for the 8080. (Intel)

8228 System controller for the 8080. (Intel)

8251 USART for the 8080 family. Also called a PCI. (Intel)

8253 Programmable interval timer for the 8080 family. (Intel)

8255 Programmable parallel interface for the 8080 family. (Intel)

8257 Direct memory access controller for the 8080 family. (Intel)

8259 Interrupt controller for the 8080 family. (Intel)

8271 Single density floppy disk controller in the 8080 family. (Intel)

8273 Synchronous data link controller in the 8080 family. (Intel)

8275 CRT controller in the 8080 family. (Intel)

8279 Keyboard and display controller in the 8080 family. (Intel)

8291 IEEE 488 bus talker/listener interface chip. (Intel)

8292 IEEE 488 bus controller chip. (Intel)

8708 See: 2708.

8748 8048 with EPROM on the same chip as the processor. (Intel)

9080 AMD's 8080.

9400 Bipolar Macrologic family. (Fairchild)

9511 Arithmetic processing chip. (AMD)

9900 16-bit microprocessor compatible with the 990 series of minicomputers. (TI)

9904 9900 clock. (TI)

9914 IEEE 488 bus interface chip. Supports talker/listener and controller functions. (TI)

9940 16-bit one-chip microcomputer with EPROM and RAM on the processor chip. (TI)

9980 16-bit byte-oriented microprocessor. (TI)

9995 9900 microprocessor with 8-bit data bus, on-chip RAM and interval timer, and high operating speed. (TI)

10696 Rockwell PIO.

10706 PPS clock. (Rockwell)

10800 Motorola ECL 4-bit slice.

10817 PPS8 DMAC. (Rockwell)

10936 PPS8 FDC. (Rockwell)

11806 Rockwell PPS8.

12660 Rockwell PPS4.

16000 Series of 16-bit microprocessors. (National Semiconductor)

16008 16-bit microprocessor with 8-bit data bus, 64K address range, and two instruction sets, one of which is that of the 16000 family, the other that of the 8080. (National Semiconductor)

16016 16-bit microprocessor with the 8080 and 16000 series instruction sets. (National Semiconductor)

16032 16-bit microprocessor with 32-bit internal architecture and 16-megabyte addressing range. (National Semiconductor)

16081 Floating-point slave processor for the 16000 series microprocessors. (National Semiconductor)

16082 Memory management unit for the 16000 series microprocessors. (National Semiconductor)

57001 New name for 5701. (MMI)

67001 New name for 6701. (MMI)

67110 Microprogram sequencer. (MMI)

68000 16-bit microprocessor with 32-bit internal structure. Features an asynchronous bus, supervisor mode operation, and an instruction set designed to support structured programming. (Motorola)

68488 IEEE 488 bus talker/listener interface chip. (Motorola)

8X300 Microcontroller. (Signetics, SMS)

F8 See: 3850, 3851.

iAPX432 32-bit, 3-chip microprocessor. Consists of an instruction-decode unit (43201), a linked micro-execution unit (43202), and and interface processor. The three chips are housed in 64-pin QUIPs and communicate on a packet bus. The iAPX432 has hardware support for multiprocessing, operating systems, and object-oriented languages. (Intel)

iAPX86   8086 family of processors and co-processors.

iAPX88   8088 family of processors and co-processors.

LSI-11   Digital Equipment Corporation LSI implementation of the PDP-11 series instruction set.

PPS-4   4-bit   microprocessor. (Rockwell)

PPS-8   8-bit   microprocessor. (Rockwell)

SC/MP   Simple   Cost-Effective Microprocessor. 8-bit microprocessor. (National Semiconductor)

TMS-1000   4-bit family of one-chip microcomputers. (TI)

Z8   8-bit one-chip microcomputer. (Zilog)

Z80   8-bit microprocessor. Upgrade of the 8080, contains extra registers and an expanded instruction set. (Zilog)

Z8000   16-bit   microprocessor with 8-megabyte segmented addressing range and supervisor operating mode. (Zilog)

Z8001   Version of the Z8000 having 8 megabyte segmented addressing range. (Zilog)

Z8002   Version of the Z8000 having only a 64K byte addressing range. (Zilog)

PART TWO

International Microcomputer Vocabulary

SECTION ONE
Danish
Dutch
French
German
Hungarian

ENGLISH	DANISH	DUTCH
A		
Acknowledge	Acknowledge	Bevestigen
Accumulator	Sumvæej	Accumulator
Aging	Foraeldelse	Veroudering
ALU	Regneenhed	Rekenorgaan
Assembler	Oversaetter	Assembleer-programma
Assign	Tildele	Toewijzen
Asynchronous	Asynkron	Asynchroon
Available	Tilgaengelig	Beschikbaar
B		
Battery	Batteri	Batterij
Bi-directional	Tovejs	Tweerichtings-
Board	Print Plade	Kaart
Bootstrap	Bootstrap	Zelfstart
Branch	Forgrene	Vertakking
Buffer	Buffer	Opvanggeheugen
Bug	Fejl	Fout
Bus	Bus	Hoofdkanaal
Byte	Oktet	(Byte)
C		
Cabinet	Skab	Kast
Cable	Ledning	Kabel
Call	Kald	Aanroep
Capacitor	Kondensator	Kondensator
Card	Kort	Kaart

FRENCH	GERMAN	HUNGARIAN
Acquittement	Bestätigen	Nyugtáz
Accumulateur	Akkumulator	Akkumulátor
Vieillissement	Alterung	Oregités
Unité Arithmetique et Logique	Zentraleinheit	Arithmetikae-Logikai Egység
Assembleur	Assembler	Assembler
Affecter	Zuteilen	Kijelöl
Asynchrone	Asynchron	Aszinkron
Disponible	Verfügbar	Rendelkezésre áll
Pile, Batterie	Batterie	Elem, Akkumulátor
Bi-directionnel	Beidseitig gerichtet	Kétirányu
Carte	Platine	Kártya
Autochargeur	Urlader	Önbetöltö
Débrachement	Verzweigung	Elágazás
Mémoire-Tampon	Puffer	Puffer
Erreur	Fehler	Hiba
Bus, Chemin	Bus	Busz, sin
Octet	Byte	Byte
Châssis, Coffret	Schrank	Szekrény
Cable	Kabel	Kábel
Appel	Aufruf	Hivás
Condensateur	Kondensator	Kapacitás
Carte	Karte	Kártya

ENGLISH	DANISH	DUTCH
Carry	Mente	Overdracht
Cartridge	Kassette	Huls
Channel	Kanal	Kanaal
Chassis	Chassis	Kast
Chip	Chip	Chip
Clock	Klokke	Klok
Command	Kommando	Bevel
Compiler	Oversætter	Kompilator
Computer		Rekenautomaat
Connector	Forbindelsesled	Stekker
Console	Konsol	Bedieningspaneel
Contact	Kontakt	Kontakt
Controller	Styreenhed	Stuureenheid
Converter	Omasæser	Omvormer
Core	Kerne (-lager)	Kern (geheugen)
CPU	Centralenhed	Centrale verwerking-seenheid
Cross-Assembler	Krydsoversætter	(Zij-assembleer-programma)
C.R.	Kortlæser	Kaartlezer
CRT	Katodestrålerør	Katodestraalbuis
Cursor	Markoer	Cursor

D

Data	Data	Gegevens
Data Collection	Dataindsamling	Inzamelen van Gegevens
Debugger	Fejlretter	Hulp bij het sporen van fouten

FRENCH	GERMAN	HUNGARIAN
Retenue	Übertrag	Atvitel
Cartouche	Magazin	«Tar», Cartridge
Canal	Kanal	Csatorna
Chassis	Chassis	Alaplemez
Pastille, «Puce»	Chip	Chip, Morzsa
Horloge	Uhr	Ora
Contrôle	Befehl	Parancs
Compilateur	Compiler	Compiler
Ordinateur	Computer	Számitógép
Connecteur	Stecker	Csatlakozó
Pupitre	Konsole	Konzol
Contact	Kontakt	Csatlakonzópont
Contrôleur	Steuergerät	Verérlo
Convertisseur	Konverter	Konverter
Tore	Kern	Mag
Unité Centrale	Zentralsteuereinheit	Központi egység
Assembleur Externe	Cross Assembler	Cross-Assembler
Lecteur de Cartes	Kartenleser	Jártyaolvasó
Console de Visualisation	Bildsichtgerät	Katódsugárcso
Curseur	Cursor	Kurzor
Données	Daten	Adat
Acquisition de Données	Datensammlung	Adatgyüjtés
Aide à la Mise au Point	Fehlerbeseitigor	Hibakereso-és javitó

ENGLISH	DANISH	DUTCH
Device	Apparat	Toestel
DIP (Dual In-line Package)	DIP	DIP
Disk	Plade	Schijf
DMA	DMA	Rechtstreekse geheugentoegang
Drive	Station	Aandrijven, aandrijving
Driver	Drivprogram	Aandrijver
Dynamic	Dynamisk	Dynamisch

E

Editor	Redigeringsprogram	Tekstbewerker
Extension card	Forlængelseskort	Verlengkaart

F

Failure	Svigt	Defekt
Fetch	Hente	Haal
File	Fil	Bestand
Flag	Flag	Aanwijzer
Flip-flop	Bistabil multivibrator	Kipschakeling
Floppy-Disk	Floopy	Soepele schijf
Formatter	Formatterer	Formateerder

G

Gate	Port	Poort
GP	Generel	Voor algemeen gebruik
Ground	Jord	Aarde

FRENCH	GERMAN	HUNGARIAN
Equipement	Vorrichtung	Berendezés
DIP	DIL	Tok Két Sor Kivezetéssel
Disque	Platte	Lemez
Accès Direct Mémoire	Direkter Speicher-zugriff	Közvetlen memóriahozzáférés
Piloter	Antrieb	Meghajtás
Amplificateur	Treiber	Meghajtó
Dynamique	Dynamisch	Dinamikus
Editeur/de Source/de Texte	Editor	Szerkesztő program
Carte Rallonge	Erweiterungskarte	Kiemelő kartya
Panne	Fehler	Hiba
Chercher en Mémoire	Holen	Utasításelővétel
Fichier	Datei	File
Indicateur	Flagge	Jelzóbit
Bascule	Flip-Flop	Bistabil
Disque Souple	Floppy Disk	Floppy Diszk
Formateur	Formatierer	Formátum beállitó
Grille, Porte	Gatter	Kapu
Général, Banalisé	Allzweck	Általános célu
Terre/Masse	Erde	Föld

ENGLISH	DANISH	DUTCH
H		
Hardware	Maskinel	Apparatuur
Hard-wired	Trådet	Bedraad
High Level Language	Højniveausprog	Hogere taal
Hole	Hul	Gat
I		
Indexed	Indiceret	Geindekseerd
Indirect	Indirekte	Onrechtstreeks
Immediate	Direkte (operand)	Onmiddellijk
Input/Output	Ind/Ud-	Invoer/Uitvoer
Instruction-Set	Ordresæt	Instructiestel
Insulation	Isolation	Isolering
Integrated Circuit (IC)	Integreret Kredsloeb	Geintegreerd Circuit
Interactive	Interaktiv	Interactief
Interface	Grænseflade	Aansluiting
Interpreter	Fortolker	Vertaler
Interrupt	Afbrydelse	Onderbreking
J		
Jump	Hop	Sprong
K		
Key	Nøgle	Sieutel, Toets
Keyboard	Tastatur	Toetsenbord

FRENCH	GERMAN	HUNGARIAN
Matériel	Hardware	Hardware
Câblé	Verdrahtet	Hazalozotl
Langage Evolué	Hohe Programmiersprache	Magasszintü nyelv
Trou	Loch	Lyuk
Indexé	Indiziert	Indexezett
Indirect	Indirekt	Közvettett
Immédiat	Unmittelbar	Közvetlen
Entrée-Sortie	Eingang/Ausgang	Bemenet/Kimenet
Répertoire d'Instruction	Befehlssatz	Utasitás-készlet
Isolement	Isolation	Elválasztás
Cirouit Intégié	Integrierter Schaltkreis	Integrált Áramkör
Interactif	Interaktiv	Interaktiv
Interface, Coupleur	Schnittstelle	Interface, Csatoló egység
Interprèteur	Interpreter	Értelmező Program
Interruption	Unterbrechung	Megszakitás
Saut	Sprung	Ugrás
Touche, Clé	Schlüssel, Taste	Billentyü
Clavier	Tastenfeld	Billentyüzet

ENGLISH	DANISH	DUTCH
L		
Layer	Lag	Laag
Level	Niveau	Peil
Library	Bibliotek	Biblioteek
Line	Linie	Lijn
Line Printer	Linieskriver	Lijnschrijver
Linker	Linker	
Load	Lade	Laad
Loader	Ladeprogram	Lader
Logical	Logisk	Logisch
Loop	Løkke	Lus
M		
Mask	Maske	Masker
Microcomputer	Mikromat	Mikrokomputer
Microprocessor	Mikroprocessor	Mikroprocessor
Monitor	Monitor	Toezichter
Moving-Head Disk	Pladelager	Schijf met Bewegende Kop
Multiplexer	Multikanal	Multiplexer
N		
Network	Net	Netwerk
Noise	Støj	Ruis
O		
Opcode	Operationskode	Bewerkingskode
Operating System	Operativ System	Beheerssysteem

FRENCH	GERMAN	HUNGARIAN
Couche	Lage, Schicht	Réteg
Niveau	Ebene	Szint
Bibliotheque	Bibliothek	Könyvtár
Ligne	Leitung, Zeile	Vonal, Sor
Imprimante	Zeilendrucker	Sornyomatató
Relogeur	Bindeglied	Csatoló Program
Charge, Chargement	Laden	Terhelés, Betöltés
Chargeur	Lader	Tölto
Logique	Logisch	Logikai
Boucle	Schleife	Hurok
Masque, Masqué	Maske	Maszk
Micro-Ordinateur	Mikrocomputer	Mikroszámitógép
Microprocesseur	Mikroprozessor	Mikroprocesszor
Moniteur	Monitor	Monitor
Disque a Tôte Mobile	Platte mit Beweglichem Kopf	Mozgófejes Lemez-Memória
Multiplexeur	Multiplexer	Multiplexer
Réseau	Netzwerk	Áramkör
Bruit	Rauschen	Zaj
Code Opération	Befehlsmode, -code	Müveleti Kód
Systéme Operatoire	Betriebs-System	Operációs Rendszer

ENGLISH	DANISH	DUTCH
Output	Uddata	Uitgang
Overlap	Overlapning	Overdekking
P		
Package	Pakke	Behuizing
Panel	Panel	Lessenaar, paneel
Paper-tape	Hulstrimmel	Ponsband
Parallel Transfer	Parallel Overfoersel	Parallelle Over-drachte
Parity	Paritet	Pariteit
Peripheral	Ydre (enhed)	Randtoestel
Pin	Ben	Pin
Plotter	Grafskriver	Tekenmachine
Pointer	Pil	Pijl
Port	Port	Poort
Power	Strøm	Vermogen
Power Failure	Spændingssvigt	Netonderbreking
Power Start	Start	Inschakeling
Power Supply	Strømforsyning	Voeding
Printed Circuit (PC)	Trykt Kredsloeb	
Priority	Prioritet	Prioriteit
Program	Program	Programma
Program Counter	Ordretæller	Programma-aanwijzer
Punch	Huller	Ponsen
R		
Rack	Stativ	Rek
RAM	RAM	Lees/Schrijfgeheugen
Range	Værdimængde	Bereik
Reader	Læser	Lezer
Real-time Clock	Sandtidsu	Tijdsklok

FRENCH	GERMAN	HUNGARIAN
Sortie	Ausgang	Kimenet
Recourvrement Partiel	Überlappen	Átlapol
Boitier	Paket	Csomag
Pupitre, Panneau	Bedienungspult	Panel, Előlap
Ruban	Lochstreifen	Papirszalag
Transfer Parallèle	Paralleler Transfer	Párhuzamos Átvitel
Parité	Parität	Paritás
Périphérique	Peripheres Gerät	Perifériás
Broche	Steckerstift	Kivezetés, Pin
Bâble Tracante	Zeichengerät	Rajzoló
Pointeur	Zeiger	Mutató
Port	Port	Csatlakozás/Port
Puissance	Leistung	Táplálás
Coupure Secteur	Stromausfall	Hálózat Kimaradás
Etablissement Secteur	Einschalten	Inditás Bekapcsoláskor
Alimentation	Spannungsversorgung	Tápegység
Circuit Imprimé	Gedruckte Schaltung	Nyomtatott Áramkör
Priorité	Priorität	Prioritás
Programme	Programm	Program
Computer Ordinal	Programmzähler	Programszámláló
Perforateur	Stanzer, stanzen	Lyukasztó
Baie	Gerätegestell	Fiók
Mémoire Vive	Schreib-Lesespeicher	Irható-olvasható Memória
Gamme	Bereich	Tartomány
Lecteur	Leser	Olvasó
Horloge Temps Réel	Echtzeituhr	Valós idejü óra

ENGLISH	DANISH	DUTCH
Reed Relay		Reedrelais
Register	Register	Register
Reliability	Pålidelighed	Betrouwbaarheid
Request	Amnodning	Aanvraag, verzoek
Restart	Genstart	Herstarten
ROM	ROM	Leesgenheugen

S

ENGLISH	DANISH	DUTCH
Saving	Gemme	Besparing
Scheduling	Scheduling	Tijdsindeling
Screen	Skaerm	Scherm
Sensor	Føler	Opnemer
Sequencing	Sekvens-	Opvolging
Sequential	Sekventiel	Sekwentieel
Serial Transfer	Serieoverførsel	Seriele Doorgave
Shared	Delt	Gedeeld
Shift	Skift	Verschuiving
Silicon	Silicium	Silicium
Simulator	Simulator	Simulator
Slot	Slids	Vak
Software	Programmel	Programmatuur
Speed	Hastighed	Snelheid
Static	Statisk	Statisch
Stack	Stak	Stapel
Start	Start	Start
State/Status	Tilstand/Status	Toestand
Subsystem	Delsystem	Deelsysteem
Switching	Skifte-	Schakelen
Synchronous	Synkron	Synchroon

FRENCH	GERMAN	HUNGARIAN
Relaise à Ampoule Scellée	Schutzgasrelais	Reed jelfogó
Registre	Register	Regiszter
Fiabilité	Zuverlässigheit	Megbizhatóság
Demande	Aufforderung	Kérés
Redémarrage	Wiederbeginn	Ujraindítás
Mémoire Morte	Festwertspeicher, Lesespeicher	Csak Olvasható Memória
Economie	Einsparung	Megorzés
Découpage du Temps	Planen	Besórolás
Écran	Abschirmung	Ernyő
Capteur	Fühler	Erzékelo
Cadencement	Aneinander-Reihend	Sorbaàillitás
Séquentiel	Sequentiell	Sorrendi
Transfert en Série	Serielle Übertragung	Soros Átvitel
Partagé	Geteilt	Osztott
Décalage, Décaler	Schieben	Léptetés
Silicium	Silizium	Szilicium
Simulateur	Simulator	Szimulátor
Emmplauement	Steckerplatz	Hely, Slot
Logiciel	Software	Software
Vitesse	Geschwindigkeit	Sebesseég
Statique	Statisch	Statikus
Pile	Stapel	Zsàk Stack
Démarrer	Start	Inditás Allapot
Etat	Zustand	Státusz
Sous-Systeme	Untersystem	Alrendszer
Commutation	Schaltend	Atkapcsolás
Synchrone	Synchron	Szindron

ENGLISH	DANISH	DUTCH
T		
Tape	Bånd	Band
Tape Driver	Båndstation	Bandaandrijving
Task	Task	Taak
Terminal	Terminal	Invoer/Uitvoereenheid
Threshold	Tærskel	Drempel
Time-sharing	Tidsdeling	Tijdsverdeling
Track	Spor	Spoor
Trap	Fælde	Val
Transfer Rate	Overførselshastighed	Overdrachtssnelheid
U		
Utility	Anlæg	Nut
V		
Vectored	Vektorielt	
Voltage	Spænding	Spanning
W		
Way	Vej	Weg
Width	Bredde	Breedte
Word	Ord	Woord
Y		
Yield	Ydelse	Opbrengst

FRENCH	GERMAN	HUNGARIAN
Bande, Ruban	Band	Szalag
Dérouleur de Bande	Bandantrieb	Szalag Egység
Tâche/Processus	Aufgabe	Feladat
Console	Terminal	Adatvégállomas, Terminál
Seuil	Schwelle	Küszöb
Temps Partagé	Time-sharing	idoosztás
Piste	Spur	Nyom
Déroutement	Falle	Csapda
Vitesse de Transfert	Transferge-Schwindigkeit	Átviteli Sebesség
Utilitaire	Dienstprogramm	Szervizprögram
Vectorisé	Vektorisiert	Vektoros
Tension	Spannung	Feszültség
Voie	Weg	Ut
Largeur	Weite	Szélesség
Mot	Wort	Szó
Taux de Composanta Opérationnels-Rendement	Ausbeute	Eredmény

International Microcomputer Vocabulary

SECTION TWO

Italian
Norwegian
Polish
Spanish
Swedish

ENGLISH	ITALIAN	NORWEGIAN
A		
Acknowledge	Acknowledge	Ack
Accumulator	Accumulatore	Akkumulator
Aging	Invecchiamento	Elding
ALU	Unitá Arithmetica e Logica	Aritmetisk enhet
Assembler	Assemblatore	Oversetter
Assign	Assegnare	Tilordne
Asynchronous	Asincrono	Asynkron
Available	Disponiblile	Tilgjengelig
B		
Battery	Batteria	Batteri
Bi-directional	Bidirezionale	Toveis
Board	Scheda	Kretsort
Bootstrap	Caricatore Iniziale	Primaerlader
Branch	Brach	Forgrene
Buffer	Buffer	Buffer
Bug	Bug (errore)	Lus
Bus	Bus	Buss
Byte	Byte	Byte
C		
Cabinet	Chassis	Kabinett
Cable	Cavo	Kabel
Call	Chiamata	Kall
Capacitor	Condensatore	Kondensator
Card	Scheda, Cartella	Kort
Carry	Carry, Riporto	Mente
Cartridge	Cartridge	Kassett
Channel	Canale	Kanal

POLISH	SPANISH	SWEDISH
Zaakceptowanie	Conocimiento	Godkanna
Akumulator	Acumulador	Åckumulator
Starzenie	Envejecimiento	Aldra
Jednostka arytmetyczno-logiczna	Unidad Aritmética Lógica	ALU
Asembler	Ensamblador	Assembler
Przydziel	Asignar	Sätta
Asynchroniczny	Asincrono	Asynkron
Dostępny	Disnonible	Tillgänglig
Bateria	Pila-Dateria	Batteri
Dwukierunkowy	Bi-direccional	Dubberlriktad
Płatka	Tarjeta/Plaqueta	Mönsterkort
Wciagacz	Cargador	Bootstrap
Gałaz, Rozgałęzienie	Ramificación	Hopp
Bufor	Memoria-Tampon	Buffert
Błąd	Bug (error)	Fel
Szyna	Buo	Buss
Bajt	Octeto	Oktad
Obudowa	Chasis	Kabinett
Kabel	Cable	Kabel
Wywołanie	Llamada	Anrop
Kondensator	Condensator	Kondensator
Karta	Tarjeta	Kort
Przeniesienie	Acarreo	Överföringssiffra
Kaseta	Cartucho	Kassett
Kanał	Canal	Kanal

ENGLISH	ITALIAN	NORWEGIAN
Chassis	Tellaio	Ramme
Chip	Chip	Flis
Clock	Orologio, Clock	Klokke
Command	Comando, Controllo	Kommando
Compiler	Compilatore	Kompilator
Computer	Calcolatore	
Connector	Connetore	Bindepunkt
Console	Console, Pannello di Comando	Konsoll
Contact	Contatto	Kontakt
Controller	Unitá di Controllo	Styreenhet
Converter	Convertitore	Omformer
Core	Nucleo	Kjerne (-lager)
CPU	CPU, Unitá Centrale	Sentralenhet
Cross-Assembler	Cross-Assembler	Krysskompilator
C.R.	Lettore di Schede	Kortleser
CRT	Video	CRT
Cursor	Cursore	Markoer
D		
Data	Dati	Data
Data Collection	Acquisizione di Dati	Datainnsamling
Debugger	Debugger	Avluser
Device	Apparato	Device
DIP	DIP	Brikke
Disk	Disco	Plate

POLISH	SPANISH	SWEDISH
Chasis	Chasis	Chasi
Frytka, Kostka	Pastilla	Bricka
Zegar	Reloj	Klocka
Rozkaz	Orden	Kommando
Kompilator	Compilador	Kompilator
Maszyna cyfrowa, Komputer	Computador	Dator
Złączać	Conector	Konnektor
Pulpit, Konsola	Cónsola	Konsol
Kontakt	Contacto	Kontakt
Kontroler, Układ sterujacy	Controlador	Kontrollenhet
Konwerter	Convertidor	Omvandlare
Rdzeń	Núcleo	Kärna
Skrośny Zbieracz	Unidad Central Ensamblador	CPU
Asembler skrośny	Ensamblador Cruzado	Korsassembler
Użytnik kart	Lectora de Tarjeta	CR
Lampa oscyloskopowa	Pantalla de Rayos Catódicos	Katodstrålerör
Kursor	Cursor	Markör
Dane	Datos	Data
Gromadzenie danych, Zbieranie danych	Adquisición de Datos	Datainsamling
Poprawnik	Corrector	Avlusare
Urzadzenie	Dispositivo	Inhet
DIP	DIP	DIP (kapsel)
Dysk	Disco	Skiva

ENGLISH	ITALIAN	NORWEGIAN
DMA	Accesso diretto alla memoria	DMA
Drive	Guidare	Stasjon
Driver	Driver	Styreprogram
Dynamic	Dinamico	Dynamisk
E		
Editor	Programma Editore	Redigeringsprogram
Extension card	Prolunga	Utvidelseskort
F		
Failure	Guasto	Svikt
Fetch	Fetch	Hente
File	File	Fil
Flag	Flag	Flagg
Flip-flop	Flip-flop	Bistabil vippe
Floppy-Disk	Floppy Disk	Diskette
Formatter	Formattatore	Formatterer
G		
Gate	Gate	Port
GP	Di uso generale	Generell
Ground	Terra	Jord
H		
Hardware	Hardware	Maskinutstyr
Hard-wired	Cablato	Fast koplet
High Level Language	Linguaggio ad alto livello	Høgnivåspåk

POLISH	SPANISH	SWEDISH
Bezpośredni dostęp do pamięci	Acceso Directo a Memoria	DMA
Sterować, Kierować		Drienhet
Zespoł napędowy	Grobernador-Controlador	
Dynamiczny	Dinámica	Dynamisk
Edytor	Editor	Textbehandlare
Karta rozszerzajaca	Carta Prolongadora	Förlängningskort
Uszkodzenie	Fallo	Fel
Pobranie	Búsqueda	Läsa
Kartoteka, Plik	Archivo	Fil
Wskaźnik	Indicador	Flagga
Przerzutnlk	Biestable	Vippa
Dysk elastyczny	Disco Flexible	Floppy disk
Formator	Conformador	Formateraro
Bramka	Puerta	Grind
Uniweroalny	Utilización General	Generell
Uziemlenie	Masa	Jord
Sprzet Material	«Hardware»	Maokinvara
Kablowany	Cableado	Hardwired
Jezyk Wyższego Rzedu	Lenguaje de Alto Nivel	Högnivåspråk

ENGLISH	ITALIAN	NORWEGIAN
Hole	Lacuna	Hull

I

Indexed	Indexato	Indeksert
Indirect	Indiretto	Indirekte
Immediate	Immediato	Direkte (operand)
Input/Output	Ingresso/Uscita	Inn-/Ut-
Instruction-Set	Repertorio di istruzioni	Instruksjonssett
Insulation	Isolamento	Isolasjon
Integrated Circuit	Circuito Integrato	Integret Krets
Interactive	Interattivo	Interaktiv
Interface	Interfaccia	Grensesnitt
Interpreter	Interprete	Fortolker
Interrupt	Interruzione	Avbrudd

J

Jump	Salto	Hopp

K

Key	Tasto	Nøkkel
Keyboard	Tastiera	Tastebord

L

Layer	Strato	Lag
Level	Livello	Nivå
Library	Libreria	Bibliotek
Line	Linea	Linje

POLISH	SPANISH	SWEDISH
Dziura	Agujero	Hål
Indeksowany	Indexado	Indexerad
Pósredni	Indirecto	Indirekt
Natychmiastowy	Immediato	Omedelbar
Wejście/Wyjście	Entrada/Salida	In/Ut
Lista Rozkazów	Instrucciones	Instruktions repetoar
Izolacja	Aislamiento	Isolering
Uzupelniony	Circuito Integrado	Integret Krets
Interakcyjnie	Interactivo	Interaktiv
Sprzeg Ztączać	Interfase	
Tlumacz	Intérprete	Interpretator
Przerwanie	Interrupcion	Avbrott
Skok	Salto	Hopp
Klucz	Tecla-Pulsador	Tangent
Klawiatura	Teclado	Tangentbord
Warstwa	Capa	Lager
Poziom	Nivel	Nivå
Biblioteka	Librería	Biblliotek
Linia, Wicrsz	Linea	Rad

ENGLISH	ITALIAN	NORWEGIAN
Line Printer	Stampante	Linjeskriver
Linker	Arracordo di Programma	Lenker
Load	Caricamento	Laste
Loader	Caricatore	Lasteprogram
Logical	Logica	Logisk
Loop	Loop	Sløyfe

M

Mask	Maschera	Máske
Microcomputer	Microcalcolatore	Mikrodatamaskin
Microprocessor	Microprocessore	Mikroprosessor
Monitor	Monitor	Monitor
Moving-Head Disk		Platelager
Multiplexer	Multiplexer	Multiplekser

N

Network	Rete	Nettverk
Noise	Distrubo, rumore	Støy

O

Opcode	Codice Operativo	Operasjonskode
Operating System	Sistema Operativo	Operativsystem
Output	Uscita	Utdata
Overlap	Overlap	Overlagring

POLISH	SPANISH	SWEDISH
Drukarka wierszowa	Impresora	Radskrivare
Ogniwo łączące	Linker (editor de enlaces)	Länkare
Wprowadzenie, Obciążenie	Carga	Enhet
Ładowacz	Cargador	Laddare
Logiczny	Lógico	Logisk
Pętla	Bucle	Snurra, Slinga
Maska	Enmascarado	Mask
Mikrokomputer	Microcomputador	Mikrodator
Mikroprocesor	Microprocesador	Mikroprocessor
Monitor	Monitor	Monitor
Dysk z ruchomymi głowicami	Cabeza Móvil	Disco a teste mobili
Multiplekser	Multiplexor	Väljare
Sieć	Red	Nät
Szum	Ruido	Brus
Kod operacyjny	Código Operación	Instruktionskod
System Operacyjny	Sistema Operativo	Operativsystem
Wyjście	Salida	Utgaång
Zakładka	Solapa	Överlappning

ENGLISH	ITALIAN	NORWEGIAN

P

English	Italian	Norwegian
Package	Programma	Pakke
Panel	Pannello	Panel
Paper-tape	Banda di Carta	Hullband
Parallel Transfer	Transmissione Parallela	Parallell Overfoering
Parity	Paritá	Paritet
Peripheral	Periferico	Ytre
Pin	Piedino	Pinne
Plotter	Diagrammatore	Plotter
Pointer	Puntatore	Peker
Port	Porta	Port
Power	Potenza	Strøm
Power-Failure	Caduta di tensione	Spenningssvikt
Power Start	Accensione	Start
Power Supply	Alimentatore	Kraftforsyning
Printed Circuit (PC)	Circuito Stampato	Trykt Krets
Priority	Prioritá	Prioritet
Program	Programma	Program
Program Counter	Program Counter	Programteller
Punch	Perforatore	Punsjemaskin

R

English	Italian	Norwegian
Rack	Telaio	Stativ
RAM	RAM	RAM
Range	Gamma	Verdiomrade
Reader	Lettore	Leser

POLISH	SPANISH	SWEDISH
Opakowanieplyta	Paquete de Programas	Paket
Panel	Panel	Panel
Taśma papierowa	Cinta de Papel	Hålremsa
Przesłanie Równoległe	Transferencia Paralela	Parallell Överföring
Kontrola Poprawności	Paridad	Paritet
Urzadzenie peryferyjne	Periférico	Periferenhet
Końcowka, Nóżka	Patilla	Ben
Pisak	Trazador	Plotter
Wskaźnik	Puntero/indicador de dirección	Pekare
Brama	Puerta/Port	Port
Moc	Potencia	Kraft
Uszkodzenie zasilanią	Fallo de Alimentación	Kraftufel
Właczenie zasilania	Puesta en Tensión	Kraft tillslag
Zasilanie	Alimentación	Kraftenhet
Obwód Drukowany	Circuito Impreso	Kretsmönster
Pierszeństwo	Prioridad	Prioritet
Program	Programa	Program
Licznik programowy	Contador de Programa	Program räknare
Perforator	Perforar	Stansa
Stojak	Bastidor	Skåp
Pamięć o dostepie swobodnym	Memoria de Acceso Aleatorio	RWM, läs-skrivminne
Zakres	Gama/intervalo	Intervall
Czytnik	Lectora	Lasare

ENGLISH	ITALIAN	NORWEGIAN
Real-time Clock	Orologio di Tempo Reale	Sanntidsklokke
Reed Relay		
Register	Registro	Register
Reliability	Affidabilità	Pålitelighet
Request	Richiesta	Anmodning
Restart	Ripartenza	Omstart
ROM	ROM	ROM

S

Saving	Risparmio	Gjemme
Scheduling	Scheduling	Scheduling
Screen	Schermo/Video	Skjerm
Sensor	Sensore	Føler
Sequencing	Sequenza	Sekvens-
Sequential	Sequenziale	Sekvensiell
Serial Transfer	Trasferimento Seriale	Seriell overføring
Shared	Ripartito	Delt
Shift	Shift	Skift
Silicon	Silicio	Silisium
Simulator	Simulatore	Simulator
Slot	Slot	Sprekk
Software	Software	Programutrustning
Speed	Velocita	Hastighet
Static	Statico	Statisk
Stack	Stack	Stack
Start	Partenza	Start

POLISH	SPANISH	SWEDISH
Zegar czasu rzeczywistego	Reloj de Tiempo Real	Healtidsklocka
Kontaktron	Relé Reed	Reed Relay
Rejestr	Registro	Register
Niezawodność	Fiabilitad	Tillförlitlighet
Zadanie	Petición	Förfrågan
Rozpocząć na nowo	Arranque	
Pamieć stata, manwa	Memoria de Sólo Lectura	Fast minne
Oszczędzanie	Guardar Control Temporal	Undam lagring
Cedulowanie	Previsión de Tiempos	Planera
Ekran	Pantalla	Bildskärm
Czujnik	Captador	Sensor
Szeregowanie	Secuencia de sucessos	Sekvensiera
Sekwencyjny	Secuencial	Sekvensleil
Przesłanie szeregowe	Transferencia Serie	Seriell transport
Dzielony	Compartido	Delad
Przesunięcie	Desplazamiento	Skift
Krzem	Siliclo	Kisel
Symulator	Simulador	Simulator
Wycięcie	Ranura	Position
Oprogramowanie	«Software»	Programvara
Szybkość	Velocidad	Hastighet
Statyczny	Estático	Statisk
Stos	Pila	Stack
Start	Arrangue	Start

ENGLISH	ITALIAN	NORWEGIAN
State/Status	Stato	Tilstand/Status
Subsystem	Sottosistema	Undersystem
Switching	Commutazione	Svitsjing
Synchronous	Sincrono	Synkron

T

Tape	Banda, Nastro	Bånd
Tape Driver	Dérouleur de Banda	Båndstasjon
Task	Attivitá	Task
Terminal	Terminale	Terminal
Threshold	Soglia	Terskel
Time-sharing	Ripartizione di Tempo	Tidsdeling
Track	Traccia	Spor
Trap	Trap	Felle
Transfer Rate	Velocita di Trasferimento	Overføringshastighet

U

Utility	di Utilita	Anlegg

V

Vectored	Vettorizzato	Vektorielt
Voltage	Tensione	Spenning

W

Way	Via	Vei
Width	Larghezza	Bredde
Word	Parola	Ord

Y

Yield	Yield	Ytelse

POLISH	SPANISH	SWEDISH
Stan	Estado	Status
Podsystem	Subsistema	Delsystems
Przełązanie	Conmutación	
Synchroniczny	Sincrónico	Synkron
Taśma	Cinta	Band
Przewijak taśmy	Controlador de Cinta	Bandspelare
Zadanje	Tarea	Process
Końcówka	Terminal	Terminal
Próg	Umbral	Tröskel
Podział czasu	Tiempo Compartido	Tidsdelning
Ścieźk, Ślad	Pista	Spår
Pułapka	Trampa	
Szybkość przesyłania	Velocidad de transferencia	Överföringshastighet
Użytkowy	Utilidad	Hjälpprogram
Wektorowy	Vectorizado	
Napięcie	Voltaje	Spänning
Droga	Via	Sätt
Szerokość	Anchura	Bredd
Słowo	Palabra	Ord
Uzysk, Wydajność	Rendimiento	Utbyte

PART THREE

Standards
and
Specifications

EIA RS-232C SIGNALS

PIN #	SYMBOL	DESCRIPTION
1		Protective chassis ground.
2	TXD	Transmit data to communication equipment.
3	RXD	Receive data from communication equipment.
4	RTS	Request to send to communication.
5	CTS	Clear to send from communication equipment.
6	DSR	Data set ready from communication equipment.
7		Signal ground.
8	DCD	Data carrier detect from communication equipment.
20	DTR	Data terminal ready to communication equipment.

IEEE 488 (GPIB, HPIB) BUS SIGNALS

CONTACT #	SYMBOL	DESCRIPTION
1-4	DIO 1-4	Data lines. Carry data.
5	EOI	End or identify. End of transfer or polling sequence.
6	DAV	Data valid. Indicates if data lines contain stable data.
7	NRFD	Not ready for data. Goes false when all devices are ready for data.
8	NDAC	Not data accepted. Goes false when all devices have accepted data.
9	IFC	Interface clear. A reset signal.
10	SRQ	Service request. Interrupt signal.
11	ATN	Attention. Indicates if data lines carry an address or data.
12	SHIELD	
13-16	DIO 5-8	Data lines. Carry data.
17	REN	Remote enable. Selects front panel operation.
18-23	Gnd 6-11	Signal ground return of contacts 6 to 11.
24	Gnd, LOGIC	

IEEE 696 (S-100) BUS SIGNALS

CONTACT#	SYMBOL*	ACTIVE LEVEL	DESCRIPTION
1	+8V		Positive 8 volts, unregulated.
2	+16V		Positive 16 volts, unregulated.
3	XRDY	H	External ready input to bus master. Bus is ready when both XRDY and RDY are true.
4	VI0	L	Vectored interrupt line 0.
5	VI1	L	Vectored interrupt line 1.
6	VI2	L	Vectored interrupt line 2.
7	VI3	L	Vectored interrupt line 3.
8	VI4	L	Vectored interrupt line 4.
9	VI5	L	Vectored interrupt line 5.
10	VI6	L	Vectored interrupt line 6.
11	VI7	L	Vectored interrupt line 7.
12	NMI	L	Non-maskable interrupt.
13	PWRFAIL	L	Power fail bus signal.
14	DMA3	L	Temporary master priority bit 3.
15	A18	H	Extended address bit 18.
16	A16	H	Extended address bit 16.
17	A17	H	Extended address bit 17.
18	SDSB	L	Status Disable. Disables line drivers for the 8 status signals.
19	CDSB	L	Control Disable. disables line drivers for the 5 control output signals.
20	GND		System ground, common with pin 100.
21	NDEF		Not to be defined.
22	ADSB	L	Address Disable. Disables the line drivers for the 16 address signals.

*Note: Control output bus signal names are prefixed with a 'p'.

Status signal names are prefixed with an 's'.

CONTACT#	SYMBOL*	ACTIVE LEVEL	DESCRIPTION
23	DODSB	L	Data Out Disable. Disables the line drivers for the 8 data output signals.
24	φ	H	Master timing signal for the bus.
25	pSTVAL	L	Status valid strobe.
26	pHLDA	H	Hold Acknowledge. Used by a permanent bus master to acknowledge a hold request for bus master transfer.
27	RFU		Reserved for future use.
28	RFU		Reserved for future use.
29	A5	H	Address bit 5.
30	A4	H	Address bit 4.
31	A3	H	Address bit 3.
32	A15	H	Address bit 15. (Most significant for non-extended addressing.)
33	A12	H	Address bit 12.
34	A9	H	Address bit 9.
35	DO1/DATA1	H	Data out bit 1, bidirectional data bit 1.
36	DO0/DATA0	H	Data out bit 0, bidirectional data bit 0.
37	A10	H	Address bit 10.
38	DO4/DATA4	H	Data out bit 4, bidirectional data bit 4.
39	DO5/DATA5	H	Data out bit 5, bidirectional data bit 5.
40	DO6/DATA6	H	Data out bit 6, bidirectional data bit 6.
41	DI2/DATA10	H	Data in bit 2, bidirectional data bit 10.
42	DI3/DATA11	H	Data in bit 3, bidirectional data bit 11.

CONTACT#	SYMBOL*	ACTIVE LEVEL	DESCRIPTION
43	DI7/DATA15	H	Data in bit 7, bidirectional data bit 15.
44	sM1	H	Status signal indicating that the current cycle is an opcode fetch.
45	sOUT	H	Status signal identifying bus cycles transferring data to an output device.
46	sINP	H	Status signal identifying bus cycles transferring data from an input device.
47	sMEMR	H	Memory Read. Status signal identifying bus cycles which transfer data from memory to a bus master and are not interrupt acknowledge instruction fetch cycles.
48	sHLTA	H	Status signal acknowledging execution of a an HLT (halt) instruction.
49	CLOCK		2 MHz 40% to 60% duty cycle clock.
50	GND		System ground, common with pin 100.
51	+8V		Positive 8 volts, unregulated. Common with pin 1.
52	−16V		Negative 16 volts, unregulated.
53	GND		System ground, common with pin 100.
54	SLAVE CLR	L	A signal to reset bus slaves. Must be active with POC, can be generated externally.
55	DMA0	L	Temporary master priority bit 0.
56	DMA1	L	Temporary master priority bit 1.
57	DMA2	L	Temporary master priority bit 2.
58	sXTRQ	L	Sixteen-bit Request. Status signal requesting 16-bit slaves to assert SIXTN.

CONTACT#	SYMBOL*	ACTIVE LEVEL	DESCRIPTION
59	A19	H	Extended address bit 19.
60	SIXTN	I	Signal generated by 16-bit slaves in response to the sixteen-bit request signal sX-TRQ, indicating that a 16-bit transfer is possible.
61	A20	H	Extended address bit 20.
62	A21	H	Extended address bit 21.
63	A22	H	Extended address bit 22.
64	A23	H	Extended address bit 23.
65	NDEF		Not to be defined.
66	NDEF		Not to be defined.
67	PHANTOM	L	A bus signal which disables normal slave devices and enables phantom slaves. Used primarily for bootstrapping systems without front panels.
68	MWRT	H	Memory write strobe. Indicates memory write bus cycles. MWRT is generated as follows: MWRT = (pWR AND NOT(sOUT))
69	RFU		Reserved for future use.
70	GND		System ground, common with pin 100.
71	RFU		Reserved for future use.
72	RDY	H	One of two ready inputs to bus master.
73	INT	I	Primary Interrupt request signal.
74	HOLD	L	Hold Request. Used by a temporary master to request control of the bus.
75	RESET	L	Resets bus master devices. Must be active with POC, and may be generated externally.
76	pSYNC	H	Control signal identifying start of bus cycle.

CONTACT#	SYMBOL*	ACTIVE LEVEL	DESCRIPTION
77	pWR	L	Write. Control signal indicating valid data on DO bus or data bus.
78	pDBIN	H	Data Bus In. Control signal requesting data on the DI bus or data bus from the currently addressed slave.
79	A0	H	Address bit 0. (least significant).
80	A1	H	Address bit 1.
81	A2	H	Address bit 2.
82	A6	H	Address bit 6.
83	A7	H	Address bit 7.
84	A8	H	Address bit 8.
85	A13	H	Address bit 13.
86	A14	H	Address bit 14.
87	A11	H	Address bit 11.
88	DO2/DATA2	H	Data out bit 2, bidirectional data bit 2.
89	DO3/DATA3	H	Data out bit 3, bidirectional data bit 3.
90	DO7/DATA7	H	Data out bit 7, bidirectional data bit 7.
91	DI4/DATA12	H	Data in bit 4, bidirectional data bit 12.
92	DI5/DATA13	H	Data in bit 5, bidirectional data bit 13.
93	DI6/DATA14	H	Data in bit 6, bidirectional data bit 14.
94	DI1/DATA9	H	Data in bit 1, bidirectional data bit 9.
95	DI0/DATA8	H	Data in bit 0, bidirectional data bit 8.
96	sINTA	H	Interrupt Acknowledge. Status signal identifying bus cycles following an accepted interrupt request presented on INT.

CONTACT#	SYMBOL*	ACTIVE LEVEL	DESCRIPTION
97	sWO	L	Write Out. Status signal identifying a bus cycle transferring data from a bus master to a slave.
98	ERROR	L	Bus status signal indicating an error condition during current bus cycle.
99	POC	L	Power-On Clear. Resets all bus devices on power-up.
100	GND		System ground.

HEXADECIMAL DIGIT CONVERSION TABLE

HEX	DECIMAL	OCTAL	BINARY
0	0	0	0000
1	1	1	0001
2	2	2	0010
3	3	3	0011
4	4	4	0100
5	5	5	0101
6	6	6	0110
7	7	7	0111
8	8	10	1000
9	9	11	1001
A	10	12	1010
B	11	13	1011
C	12	14	1100
D	13	15	1101
E	14	16	1110
F	15	17	1111

THE ASCII CHARACTER SET

CODE	CHAR	CODE	CHAR	CODE	CHAR	CODE	CHAR
0	NUL	32[1]		64	@	96[5]	`
1	SOH	33	!	65	A	97	a
2	STX	34	"	66	B	98	b
3	ETX	35	#	67	C	99	c
4	EOT	36	$	68	D	100	d
5	ENQ	37	%	69	E	101	e
6	ACK	38	&	70	F	102	f
7	BEL	39[2]	'	71	G	103	g
8	BS	40	(	72	H	104	h
9	TAB	41	)	73	I	105	i
10	LF	42	*	74	J	106	j
11	VT	43			75	K	107	k
12	FF	44[3]	,	76	L	108	l
13	CR	45	—	77	M	109	m
14	SO	46	.	78	N	110	n
15	SI	47	/	79	O	111	o
16	DLE	48	0	80	P	112	p
17	DC1	49	1	81	Q	113	q
18	DC2	50	2	82	R	114	r
19	DC3	51	3	83	S	115	s
20	DC4	52	4	84	T	116	t
21	NAK	53	5	85	U	117	u
22	SYN	54	6	86	V	118	v
23	ETB	55	7	87	W	119	w
24	CAN	56	8	88	X	120	x
25	EM	57	9	89	Y	121	y
26	SUB	58	:	90	Z	122	z
27	ESC	59	;	91	[	123	{
28	FS	60	<	92	\	124		
29	GS	61	=	93	]	125[6]	}
30	RS	62	>	94	↑	126	~
31	US	63	?	95[4]	_	127[7]	DEL

[1]space	[3]comma	[5]grave accent	[7]or RUBOUT
[2]single quote	[4]or back arrow	[6]or ALT MODE	

PART FOUR

Microcomputer Companies

SUPPLIERS OF MICROCOMPUTER
SYSTEMS AND COMPONENTS

Advanced Micro Devices, Inc.
901 Thompson Place
Sunnyvale, CA 94086
(408) 732-2400

Alpha Micro Systems
17881 Sky Park North
Irvine, CA 92713
(714) 957-1404

Altos Computer Systems
2360 Bering Drive
San Jose, CA 95131

American Microsystems Inc.
3800 Homestead Road
Santa Clara, CA 95051
(408) 246-0330

Apple Computer, Inc.
10260 Bandley Drive
Cupertino, CA 95014
(408) 996-1010

Atari, Inc.
1265 Borregas Ave.
P.O. Box 427
Sunnyvale, CA 94086

Burr-Brown
International Airport Industrial Park
P.O. Box 11400
Tucson, AZ 85734
(602) 294-1431

Commodore Business Machines
3330 Scott Blvd.
Santa Clara, CA 95051
(408) 946-7700

Cromemco
280 Bernardo Ave.
Mountain View, CA 94043
(415) 964-7400

Data General
Route 9
Westboro, MA 01772
(617) 366-8911

Diablo Systems Inc.
24500 Industrial Blvd.
Hayward, CA 94545
(415) 786-5000

Digital Equipment Corp.
146 Main St.
Maynard, MA 01754
(617) 897-5111

Digital Research
P.O. Box 579
Pacific Grove, CA 93950

Dynabyte
1005 Elwell Court
Palo Alto, CA 94303
(415) 965-1010

Electronic Arrays
550 East Middlefield Road
Mountain View, CA 94043
(415) 964-4321

Electronic Memories & Magnetics
12624 Daphne Ave.
Hawthorne, CA 90250
(213) 777-4070

Exidy Systems, Inc.
1234 Elko Drive
Sunnyvale, CA 94086

Fairchild Camera & Instrument
464 Ellis Street
Mountain View, CA 94040
(415) 962-3336

Fairchild Semiconductor
1725 Technology Drive
San Jose, CA 95110
(408) 998-0123

**General Instrument Micro-
    electronics**
600 West John Street
·Hicksville, NY 11802
(516) 733-3107

Godbout Electronics
P.O. Box 2355
Oakland Airport
Oakland, CA 94614
(415) 562-0636

Harris Semiconductor
625 Ellis Street 3300
Mountain View, CA 94043
(415) 964-6443

Heath Co.
Hilltop Road
Benton Harbor, MI 49022

Hewlett-Packard
3404 East Harmony Rd.
Fort Collins, CO 80525
(303) 226-3800

Hitachi America, Ltd.
1800 Bering Drive
San Jose, CA 95112
(408) 292-6404

Hughes Solid State Products
500 Superior Avenue
Newport Beach, CA 92663
(714) 759-2411

IBM (personal computers)
425 Market St.
San Francisco, CA 94119
(415) 525-2000

IMS Associates, Inc.
910 81st Ave.
Bldg. 14
Oakland, CA 94621

Inmos
P.O. Box 16000
Colorado Springs, CO 80935
(303) 603-4000

Intel
3065 Bowers Avenue
Santa Clara, CA 95051
(408) 987-8080

International Rectifier Corp.
233 Kansas St.
El Segundo, CA 90345
(213) 772-2000

Intersil, Inc.
10670 N. Tantau Ave.
Cupertino, CA 95014
(408) 996-5000

Intertec Data Systems
2300 Broad River Road
Columbia, SC 29210

Ithaca Intersystems, Inc.
1650 Hanshaw Road
Ithaca, NY 14850
(607) 257-7733

ITT Semiconductor
175C New Boston Street
Woburn, MA 01801
(617) 935-6750

Lifeboat Associates
1661 Third Ave.
New York, NY 10028
(212) 860-0300

Micro Pro International Corp.
1299 4th St.
San Rafael, CA 94901
(415) 457-8990

Microsoft Consumer Products
10800 Northeast Eighth, Suite 819
Bellevue, WA 98004
(206) 455-8000

Monolithic Memories, Inc.
1165 East Arques Avenue
Sunnyvale, CA 94086
(408) 739-3535

Morrow Designs
5221 Central Ave.
Richmond, CA 94804
(415) 524-2101

MOS Technology
950 Rittenhouse Road
Norristown, PA 19401
(215) 666-7950

Mostek Corporation
1215 West Crosby Road
Carrollton, TX 75006
(214) 323-1552

Motorola Semiconductor
P.O. Box 20912
Phoenix, AZ 85036
(602) 244-6900

National Semiconductor
2900 Semiconductor Drive
Santa Clara, CA 95051
(408) 733-2600

NEC Electronics USA, Inc.
550 East Middlefield Road
Mountain View, CA 94043
(415) 964-4321

North Star Computers, Inc.
14440 Catalina
San Leandro, CA
(415) 357-8500

OKI Semiconductor
Suite 405, 1333 Lawrence
    Expressway
Santa Clara, CA 95051
(408) 984-4840

Onyx Systems, Inc.
73 East Trimble Road
San Jose, CA 95131
(408) 946-6330

Osborne Computer Corp.
26500 Corporate Dr.
Hayward, CA 94545
(415) 887-8080

Peachtree Software
3 Corporate Square 3700
Atlanta, GA 30329

Personal Software, Inc.
1330 Bordeaux Drive
Sunnyvale, CA 94086
(408) 745-7841

Phase One Systems, Inc.
7700 Edgewater Dr. 3830
Oakland, CA 94621
(415) 562-8085

Plessey Semiconductor
1641 Kaiser Ave.
Irvine, CA 92714
(714) 540-9979

Precision Monolithics, Inc.
1500 Space Park Drive
Santa Clara, CA 95050
(418) 246-9222

Qume Corp.
2323 Industrial Parkway West
Hayward, CA 94545
(408) 942-4000

Radio Shack
1300 One Tandy Center
Fort Worth, TX 76102
(817) 390-3272

Raytheon Semiconductor
350 Ellis St.
Mountain View, CA 94042
(415) 968-9211

RCA Solid State
P.O. Box 3200
Somerville, NJ 08876
(201) 685-6000

Rockwell International
3310 Miraloma Avenue
P.O. Box 3669
Anaheim, CA 92803
(714) 632-3729

Scientific MicroSystems
777 East Middlefield Rd.
Mountain View, CA 94043
(415) 964-5700

SGS Ates
240 Bear Hill Road
Waltham, MA 02154
(617) 890-6688

Sharp
10 Keystone Place
Paramus, NJ 07652
(201) 265-5600

Shugart Associates
435 Oakmead Parkway
Sunnyvale, CA 94086
(408) 733-0100

Siemens Corporation
P.O. Box 1000
Iselin, NJ 08830

Signetics
811 East Arques Avenue
Sunnyvale, CA 94086
(408) 739-7700

Sinclair Research, Ltd.
One Sinclair Plaza
Nashua, NH 03061

Solid State Devices, Inc.
14000 Valley View Avenue
La Mirada, CA 90638
(213) 921-9660

**Southwest Technical Products
  Corp.**
219 W Rhapsody
San Antonio, TX 78216

Structured Systems Group, Inc.
5204 Claremont Ave.
Oakland, CA 94018
(415) 547-1567

Synertek, Inc.
3001 Stender Way
Santa Clara, CA 95051
(408) 988-5611

Tarbell Electronics
950 Dovlen Place 313
Carson, CA 90746
(213) 538-4251

Tektronix, Inc.
P.O. Box 4828
Portland, OR 97208

Texas Instruments
P.O. Box 1443
Houston, TX 77001
(713) 490-2000

Thunderware, Inc.
P.O. Box 13322
Oakland, CA 94661

Toshiba America
2151 Michelson Drive, Suite 190
Irvine, CA 92715
(714) 955-1155

TRW LSI Products
P.O. Box 2472
La Jolla, CA 92038
(714) 578-5990

Verbatim Corp.
323 Soquel Way
Sunnyvale, CA 94086
(418) 245-4400

Vodex—A Votrax Company
500 Stephenson Highway
Troy, MI 48084

Western Digital Corporation
3128 Redhill Ave., Box 2180
Newport Beach, CA 92663
(714) 557-3550

Xerox Corporation
Technical Information Center
323 Coyote Hill Road
Palo Alto, CA 94304
(415) 494-4000

Zilog, Inc.
10340 Bubb Road
Cupertino, CA 95014
(408) 446-4666

MICROCOMPUTER PERIODICALS

Byte and **Popular
Computing**
70 Main Street
Peterborough, NH 03458
(603) 924-9281

Computer Magazine
P.O. Box 5406
Greensboro, NC 27403
(919) 275-9809

Creative Computing
P.O. Box 789-M
Morristown, NJ 07960
(201) 540-0445

Datamation Magazine
666 Fifth Avenue
New York, NY 10019

Info World
530 Lytton Avenue
Palo Alto, CA 94301
(415) 328-4602

Interface Age
16704 Marquardt Avenue
Cerritos, CA 90701

Kilobaud Microcomputing
and **80 Microcomputing**
80 Pine Street
Peterborough, NH 03458
(609) 924-3873

MICRO: The 6502 Journal
P.O. Box 6502
Chelmsford, MA 01824
(617) 256-5515

**People's Computer Company
(Dr. Dobb's Journal, Recreational
   Computing,**
PCNET, Computertown USA)
1263 El Camino Real
P.O. Box E
Menlo Park, CA 94025

Robotics Age Magazine
P.O. Box 801
La Canada, CA 91011

UCSD p-System User's Society
(newsletter and library)
P.O. Box 1148
La Jolla, CA 92038

The SYBEX Library

BASIC EXERCISES FOR THE APPLE®
by J. P. Lamoitier 250 pp., 90 illustr., Ref. 0-084
This book is an Apple version of *Fifty BASIC Exercises*.

BASIC EXERCISES FOR THE IBM® PERSONAL COMPUTER
by J. P. Lamoitier 252 pp., 90 illustr., Ref. 0-088
This book is an IBM version of *Fifty BASIC Exercises*.

BASIC EXERCISES FOR THE ATARI®
by J.P. Lamoitier 251 pp., illustr., Ref. 0-101
This the ATARI version of *Fifty BASIC Exercises*.

INSIDE BASIC GAMES
by Richard Mateosian 348 pp., 120 illustr., Ref. 0-055
Teaches interactive BASIC programming through games. Games are written in Microsoft BASIC and can run on the TRS-80, Apple II and PET/CBM.

YOUR FIRST BASIC PROGRAM
by Rodnay Zaks 150 pp., illustr., Ref. 0-092
A fully illustrated, easy to use, introduction to BASIC programming. Will have the reader programming in a matter of hours.

BASIC FOR BUSINESS
by Douglas Hergert 224 pp., 15 illustr., Ref. 0-080
A logically organized, no-nonsense introduction to BASIC programming for business applications. Includes many fully-explained accounting programs, and shows you how to write them.

EXECUTIVE PLANNING WITH BASIC
by X. T. Bui 196 pp., 19 illustr., Ref. 0-083
An important collection of business management decision models in BASIC, including Inventory Management (EOQ), Critical Path Analysis and PERT, Financial Ratio Analysis, Portfolio Management, and much more.

BASIC PROGRAMS FOR SCIENTISTS AND ENGINEERS
by Alan R. Miller 318 pp., 120 illustr., Ref. 0-073
This second book in the "Programs for Scientists and Engineers" series provides a library of problem-solving programs while developing proficiency in BASIC.

CELESTIAL BASIC: Astronomy on Your Computer
by Eric Burgess 300 pp., 65 illustr., Ref. 0-087
A collection of BASIC programs that rapidly complete the chores of typical astronomical computations. It's like having a planetarium in your own home! Displays apparent movement of stars, planets and meteor showers.

PASCAL

INTRODUCTION TO PASCAL (Including UCSD Pascal™)
by Rodnay Zaks   420 pp., 130 illustr., Ref. 0-066
A step-by-step introduction for anyone wanting to learn the Pascal language.
Describes UCSD and Standard Pascals. No technical background is assumed.

THE PASCAL HANDBOOK
by Jacques Tiberghien   486 pp., 270 illustr., Ref. 0-053
A dictionary of the Pascal language, defining every reserved word, operator,
procedure and function found in all major versions of Pascal.

APPLE® PASCAL GAMES
by Douglas Hergert and Joseph T. Kalash   372 pp., 40 illustr., Ref. 0-074
A collection of the most popular computer games in Pascal, challenging the reader
not only to play but to investigate how games are implemented on the computer.

INTRODUCTION TO THE UCSD p-SYSTEM™
by Charles W. Grant and Jon Butah   300 pp., 10 illustr., Ref. 0-061
A simple, clear introduction to the UCSD Pascal Operating System; for beginners
through experienced programmers.

PASCAL PROGRAMS FOR SCIENTISTS AND ENGINEERS
by Alan R. Miller   374 pp., 120 illustr., Ref. 0-058
A comprehensive collection of frequently used algorithms for scientific and technical applications, programmed in Pascal. Includes such programs as curve-fitting,
integrals and statistical techniques.

DOING BUSINESS WITH PASCAL
by Richard Hergert & Douglas Hergert   371 pp., illustr., Ref. 0-091
Practical tips for using Pascal in business programming. Includes design considerations, language extensions, and applications examples.

OTHER LANGUAGES

FORTRAN PROGRAMS FOR SCIENTISTS AND ENGINEERS
by Alan R. Miller   280 pp., 120 illustr., Ref. 0-082
Third in the "Programs for Scientists and Engineers" series. Specific scientific and
engineering application programs written in FORTRAN.

A MICROPROGRAMMED APL IMPLEMENTATION
by Rodnay Zaks   350 pp., Ref. 0-005
An expert-level text presenting the complete conceptual analysis and design of an
APL interpreter, and actual listing of the microcode.

FOR A COMPLETE CATALOG
OF OUR PUBLICATIONS

U.S.A.
2344 Sixth Street
Berkeley,
California 94710
Tel: (415) 848-8233
Telex: 336311

SYBEX

SYBEX-EUROPE
4 Place Félix-Eboué
75583 Paris Cedex 12
France
Tel: 1/347-30-20
Telex: 211801

SYBEX-VERLAG
Heyestr. 22
4000 Düsseldorf 12
West Germany
Tel: (0211) 287066
Telex. 08 588 163